MACHIAVELLI for MOMS

Maxims on the Effective Governance of Children

SUZANNE EVANS

A TOUCHSTONE BOOK

Published by Simon & Schuster

New York   London   Toronto   Sydney   New Delhi

★ Touchstone
A Division of Simon & Schuster, Inc.
1230 Avenue of the Americas
New York, NY 10020

First Touchstone hardcover edition April 2013

TOUCHSTONE and colophon are registered trademarks of
Simon & Schuster, Inc.

For information about special discounts for bulk purchases,
please contact Simon & Schuster Special Sales at 1-866-506-1949
or business@simonandschuster.com.

The Simon & Schuster Speakers Bureau can bring authors to
your live event. For more information or to book an event contact
the Simon & Schuster Speakers Bureau at 866-248-3049 or visit our
website at www.simonspeakers.com.

Designed by Aline C. Pace

Manufactured in the United States of America

10 9 8 7 6 5 4 3 2 1

Library of Congress Cataloging-in-Publication Data is available.

ISBN 978-1-4516-9950-0
ISBN 978-1-4516-9959-3 (ebook)

With love to my kids
And with gratitude to Machiavelli,
for helping me reign them in

CONTENTS

Part I: The Experiment Begins

CONTENTS

Part II: The Experiment Goes Awry

Part III: Finding My Way Home

Appendices

PART I

The Experiment Begins

This story was born out of chaos and crisis. It's about how a totally frazzled and stressed-out mom applied the strategies of warfare and statecraft prescribed in *The Prince* to raise a happy, well-mannered family. It's also about how out of that strategy was born a more relaxed, enlightened, and well-mannered mom. At least at first . . .

I

The Prince and the Promise:
Or, What Machiavelli Can Do for You

What if I told you that your children—yes, *your* children, the ones currently jumping on their beds, slamming doors, tossing fistfuls of cereal on the floor, and bickering, whining, shrieking, fighting, or otherwise trying to kill each other—could be well behaved?

Not just "well behaved," but really and truly obedient and good.

And not only that—they would enjoy being good. And you would enjoy your time with them, instead of feeling chronically exhausted and enslaved by the impossibly wide array of demands that press in upon you each day as a parent. You know what I'm talking about: those relentless demands on your time, your energy, your finances, your sleep, and your patience, demands on your career, your figure, your friendships, and other important relationships.

What if I told you that there was a new approach, or master plan, that wouldn't just show you how to empower yourself as a parent, but how to keep that power and use it to help your kids:

- feel more confident and in control of their life . . . and help you feel happier and more relaxed;

- consistently obey your commands . . . without you having to nag;

- appreciate the value of money and hard work . . . and help you save lots of cash;

- master bad habits like back talk and procrastination . . . and help you take action;

- eagerly complete their homework . . . without your having to ask;

- battle boredom with creativity and imagination . . . without your having to entertain them;

- sleep soundly through the night . . . while you regain your sanity, sex drive, and peace of mind.

Most amazingly, what if I promised you that if you use this plan, you will find your own thoughts and feelings about parenting begin to change.

- You will feel more confident, powerful, proactive, and competent.

- You will get more out of your kids with less fight.

- You will stop daydreaming about vacationing alone in Mexico, get your healthy glow back, and might actually put off getting your tubes tied just yet.

Whether you're a stay-at-home-mom (or dad) or a highly driven career woman, stuck in a rut or searching for a new perspective, this plan will inspire you to take back your power . . . and take back your kingdom.

I thought it was a fairy tale, too. Until I tried the concepts outlined here, which I stumbled across more or less by accident in a five-hundred-year-old tome. I discovered these ideas in a moment of crisis. On the surface, it might have looked like I had everything a mom could want. My kids were healthy. My husband was hardworking, loving, and fun. We lived in a nice home in a neighborhood that I loved. I even had the most coveted and highly prized parental commodity of all: a reliable babysitter.

But . . . no one (except my babysitter) was behaving—not even my cat, who had suddenly developed a strong aversion to kitty litter. My house wasn't just a disaster; it was a battle zone, so much so that if city commissioners had dropped by for a surprise visit they would've had to clean it before they condemned it. And as much as I really do cherish and love my children, I was overwhelmed, exhausted, and out of shape, and I had worn the same tattered old expandable-waist post-pregnancy sweatpants every day since my last set of contractions kicked in.

So it was at a very low point in my life that I stumbled

across a copy of Machiavelli's *The Prince*. And reading it literally changed my life. Sounds strange, right? But his advice gave me the clarity to see my relationship with my kids in a dynamic new light. Instead of abdicating my power as a parent, I reclaimed it. Instead of struggling each day just to survive, I took command of my life. Instead of begging my kids to be courteous, polite, respectful, and kind; quickly fall into line; and stop drawing on our walls with my Pretty Please MAC lipstick, I insisted on it. And as I continued reading, I felt myself undergo a transformation from a totally beleaguered and defeated modern-day mom to a more peaceful, calm, and enlightened one.

It didn't happen overnight. And it didn't happen without some serious bumps along the way (as you'll see). I ended up taking a lot of Machiavelli's advice to heart, leaving a little bit on the table, and interpreting other parts rather broadly. But while I started this experiment in a somewhat tentative and haphazard way, I really did find kernels of truth in *The Prince* that helped me to be a better parent. I hope you will, too.

But instead of asking you to read Machiavelli's iconic book yourself (though I totally recommend it—seriously, it's a great read), I will do you one better: I will show you how to use his rules to raise a happier, better-behaved family. Really. I wouldn't kid you about something as serious as this. And because this approach worked well for me, I encourage you to try to it, too. But if you do, remember this piece of advice: don't be afraid of your power as a parent. Embrace it—then use it wisely, consistently, and, above all, lovingly.

Good luck!

II

My Machiavellian Moment:
Or, Why I Ever Thought This
Experiment Would Be a Good Idea

It was in Southern California, the early years of the twenty-first century, and I was facing an intense moment of crisis. Newly remarried, my husband, Eric, and I had moved in together with our kids and were trying to blend our family. From the beginning, it was total chaos. Not only had we not set any ground rules for trying to govern our family, we hadn't even established any ground rules for our marriage.

I know. Great plan, right? So somehow (I'm still not quite sure how it happened), virtually all of the household chores fell by default to me. This included all the grocery shopping, the cooking and cleaning, the drop-offs to and pickups from preschool, and all the carpooling, bathing, bill paying, laundry, and diaper changing. At the same time, I was trying to finish the dissertation I was writing as the final requirement for my PhD in history at UC Berkeley, and I had just started a demanding new full-time job writing legal briefs from home.

All of which meant that I was trapped (read: imprisoned!) inside for days at a time with my four rambunctious young kids, whose constant bickering was driving me nuts.

Oh, did I skip that part? Four children. Under the age of eight.

Don't get me wrong: I love my kids dearly and would walk to the far ends of Dante's Nine Circles of Hell and back on their behalf. But they also have the uncanny ability to drive me to the brink of insanity.

At six, Teddy, my oldest and most independent if sensitive daughter, would sometimes mimic me by screaming at her siblings when they irritated her with their silly childhood pranks. *"Stop following me! Leave me alone! I can't take it anymore!"* she'd howl as they giggled while trying to cuddle up next to her on the couch.

Complicating matters was the fact that I share custody of Teddy with my ex-husband, Paul. He hasn't remarried and doesn't have any other kids, which means that he can shower his undivided attention and affection on her in a way that I never can. Plus, whenever she stays with him, his peaceful, well-ordered home is her own little kingdom, where she can reign as she sees fit without so much as a hint of internal subversion or opposition. No one sneaks into her room to steal her beloved white furless stuffed kitten (more about that disaster later). No one rifles through her backpack and tears up her carefully completed homework (more on that epic battle later, too).

Which brings me to my then-three-and-a-half-year-old daughter, Katie. Katie has Down syndrome and is happiness personified. But she can also be infuriatingly stubborn and defiant. Some of her defiance was actually quite impressive in terms of originality, concept, execution, and the sheer creative destructiveness of it. And had she been performing in some sort of early-childhood-drive-your-mommy-totally-insane competition, I would've given her a perfect 10. A virtual gold medal winner in insubordination.

Katie is also an accomplished escape artist (more on that little trick later, too). Whenever I took my eyes off her to, say, grab a quick two-minute shower or search for my cell phone, which she had turned off and surreptitiously hidden under the sofa cushions, she'd spring like a fox into action and find something even more cunning and crafty to do.

Meanwhile, her trusty coconspirator was her younger brother, Trevor, who was firmly entrenched in the midst of his Terrible Twos and had a tendency to throw earth-shattering tantrums whenever our cat Lucky managed to escape from his grasp or he otherwise didn't get *exactly* what he wanted and *exactly* when he wanted it.

On top of that, my seven-year-old stepson, Daniel, wanted nothing to do with me. Whenever Eric would disappear from his view for a second or two, he'd rush around the house in a frenzied panic, shouting, "Dad! . . . Dad!! . . . DAD!!! . . . DAAAD!!! . . . DAAAAD!!! . . . DAAAAAD!!!! Then he'd return from his search, look at me, and calmly ask, "Do you know where my dad is?" To which I would usually shrug and mumble something like "I don't know, but I do know he's *not* in the laundry room, right?"

These behaviors weren't sufficient to trigger a maternal breakdown, but, in the aggregate, they made me resent motherhood and question my fitness as a parent.

"I'm a terrible mother," I'd mutter to myself as I changed yet another diaper and dreamed of the day they were all safely away at college. Then I'd feel guilty for wishing their childhood away.

Still, I desperately wanted to mold them into less irritating little creatures whose constant bickering didn't drive me to drink, who didn't suck every ounce of energy out of me with their constant needs, who were more obedient little people who would quickly and predictably submit to my parental commands.

So, like millions of other modern moms, I ignored centuries of wise advice and tried to change them—by yelling, nagging, or ignoring them. This, of course, only made their behavior worse. They'd argue a little louder, slam doors harder, and leave dirty glasses and plates on the table with greater frequency.

One night, after washing the dishes and tucking our kids into bed, I talked to my husband about the mindnumbingly tedious and oppressively isolating tyranny of motherhood. He didn't understand what I was complaining about and said that staying home all day sounded "great" to him—ha!

"Why don't you take the kids to the park if you're

going stir-crazy in the house?" he helpfully suggested one cold rainy evening.

"The park?" I said sharply. "Why don't *you* take them to the park?"

After a heated exchange, Eric made a hasty retreat to our bedroom and turned on the TV as I stomped off to my office. Too exhausted to work, I sat at my desk and stared at a dusty old shelf of books. It was practically buckling under the weight of dozens and dozens of volumes on history and literature and philosophy that were piled up high upon one another in no particular order of importance.

Even my bookshelf's a mess, I thought.

And, as I began straightening it, an old copy of *The Prince* caught my eye. You remember *The Prince*, right? Maybe you read it in high school or college, like I did. Maybe it's even moldering away on some dusty old shelf in your basement or study, too. I'd probably cast my glance over that bookshelf a thousand times over the last few years, but this time this particular volume caught my eye.

Pulling it from the shelf, I studied its cover—a portrait of Niccolò Machiavelli dressed in his elegant robes of office. His intelligent, determined eyes stared out humbly at me; his thin lips turned up in a slight, knowing smile; his stance calm, relaxed, powerful, and confident—everything that I was not at that particular point in my life.

Mesmerized, I stared at his beguiling countenance for a while, then opened the book and began reading. I had a vague idea of Machiavelli—his name, after all, is synonymous with duplicity, deceit, and the cunning and ruthless use of power. I also knew that his most famous saying is "The ends justify the means."

But what, exactly, does he mean by this? I wondered.

I wasn't sure. So, still too frazzled and mad to go to bed, I decided to sit down and flip through Machiavelli's slim volume right there and then. And as I started reading, the less tired and more excited I became because what soon became clear is that for some five hundred years this Machiavelli guy has gotten a bad rap. In fact, some scholars believe he probably never said that infamous phrase about the ends justifying the means—and even if he did, his "ends" isn't acquiring power for the sake of power itself. His goal was actually to acquire and preserve power so as to secure the safety and stability of a state. It's this stability that helps a prince ensure the happiness and well-being of his subjects.

Hmm, I thought, a stable and safe home? Full of happy and prosperous subjects? Sounds like a pretty good plan, I thought, for both a prince and a parent. And that's when I got really excited. Maybe I could use Machiavelli's rules to help me reclaim my kingdom and make my children better behaved.

As it turns out, Machiavelli began writing *The Prince* when he was in the midst of a crisis similar to mine (okay, maybe that's a slight exaggeration). But we were both at stressful, critical times in our own lives. For Machiavelli, it was in Florence, Italy, in 1513. Recently fired from his job as a high-ranking diplomat in the Florentine republic, he was unjustly arrested, imprisoned, and repeatedly tortured for his alleged role in a conspiracy to assassinate Cardinal Giuliano de' Medici and seize the government by force.

Upon his release, things went from bad to worse. Not only had the republic he had faithfully served for fourteen years fallen under the rule of tyrants, he was now barred from government service (the only career he had ever known), banished from his beloved Florence (the city, he once confessed, that he loved more than his own soul), and, in what was perhaps the most emotionally tumultuous turn of events, exiled and sent to live in the Tuscan countryside with his wife and six rambunctious young kids.

Okay, so maybe his problems were a bit more serious than mine. But what we shared was a sense of self-pity and despair at our lot in the world. So what did Machiavelli do? He wallowed in misery for a while, then began plotting his return to public life. Struggling to support his young family, burning with unfulfilled ambition, and totally bored out of his gourd, he resolved to swallow his pride and write a little primer on politics—"this little study of mine," he dismissively called it—in hopes of gaining favor among the Medicis and obtaining a new government job. And so it was that out of Machiavelli's intense moment of crisis was born *The Prince*, the most revolutionary and widely maligned political tract of all time.

Struggling to support his young family? Frustrated and bored? Sounds familiar, I thought. And by the time I finished reading *The Prince* that night, I was inspired to try a little experiment. Why not try to apply Machiavelli's rules for a successful kingdom to my life as a mom.

Sounds weird, I know. But, at its core, *The Prince* is more than just theory. In fact, it addressed an immediate political crisis that Machiavelli had seen with his own eyes—the disunity and ruin of Italy—and was meant to be a practical "how-to" book. A pragmatic master plan. A pithy and pungent no-holds-barred call to action for a cunning and ruthless new ruler to create a strong, unified state—one that would serve the common interests and ambitions of the people in their longing for power, glory, and wealth.

As I thought about this, I realized that all these concepts had great application in my life. Because when I replaced "disunity and ruin of Italy" with "disunity and ruin of my family" and substituted "parent" for "prince," it hit me that Machiavelli's little primer on politics could also be used as a parenting manifesto—a pithy and pungent, no-holds-barred call to action for me to create a stronger, more unified family aimed at satisfying the ambitions and best interests of my kids, with a few Razors, Beyblades, and Webkinz thrown in.

Yes, I was desperate for guidance. But truthfully, very few parenting books that I had read in recent years had spoken to me. I have no close family ties that I know of in China. I have no immediate plans to move to France. I know for a fact that I've never had the happiest baby or toddler on the block. And despite Dr. Spock's kindly if antiquated assurance that "we know more than we think we know" as parents, all I knew was that I didn't know much of anything other than that I felt totally frazzled and incompetent as a mom more often than not. Worse, I wasn't enjoying the time that I had with my kids—I was enduring it.

And so maybe that's why Machiavelli's manifesto on power politics—and power parenting, by extension—spoke to me in such a strange and startling way. Or maybe after changing diapers every day for the better part of a decade, playing Machiavellian mind games helped keep my brain from turning to mush. With a little imagination (and maybe one too many late-night glasses of wine), I began to see parallels between a sixteenth-century Florentine prince and twenty-first-century motherhood and quickly became convinced that the same strategies of warfare and statecraft that Machiavelli prescribed could also be applied to my kids.

Being permissive and nice didn't work. Begging, bartering, nagging, harassing, or even politely asking didn't work. But perhaps a pragmatic, tough-minded Machiavellian strategy just might! That was my theory, at least, as I set out to break free from my bonds of maternal misery to become a full-fledged, card-carrying Machiavellian Mom. As you'll see, this little experiment, this risky family adventure, had its ups . . . and its downs.

III

It Is Dangerous to Be Overly Generous:
A Good Ruler Sets Limits

So, one of the first things I learned as I read *The Prince* is that Machiavelli had a dark and pessimistic view of human nature. In what ways? Well, he observes that men are generally fickle, hypocritical, greedy, and deceitful and that their loyalties can be won and lost. To guard against shifting allegiances, Machiavelli says that a prince must develop a reputation for generosity and goodness. However, he is careful to caution that if a prince is overly generous, he will lose civic appreciation and only increase his subjects' greed for more.

The same holds true for my kids. Like all moms, I was struggling to meet their every need, to fulfill their every demand. Yet, after I read *The Prince*, I realized that the more material things I gave them, the more they expected and the less grateful they became. If I gave one scoop of ice cream to Daniel, he'd ask for two. If I carefully prepared three chicken nuggets each for Trevor and Katie, they'd demand five. And if I bought a new toy for Teddy, she'd grab it and grunt without saying "thank you." Then she'd play with it for eight seconds, toss it aside, and whine, "Where's *Daddy*? He's more fun than *you*!"

Precious moments like these made me realize that Machiavelli's maxim "It's dangerous for a prince to be overly generous" has great relevance in this increasingly materialistic world in which we live, one in which billions of marketing dollars are spent each year in a frenzied attempt to get our otherwise sweet, innocent kids to not only want but *insist* on having the latest technological gadgets and games—games, I might add, that are instantaneously outdated and replaced by thousands if not millions of more "hip" and ridiculously expensive ones.

The only way out of this trap, I thought, this relentless and seemingly endless parental guilt trip, was to channel Machiavelli and finally tighten my purse straps. Excited by this idea, I decided to apply Machiavelli's advice to my unsuspecting young subjects when they accompanied me on a trip to Target.

Usually, on outings like these, my little angels would greedily toss DVDs and dolls into our cart without asking or even giving it a thought. And—of course—when I insisted that they remove the booty, temper tantrums would swiftly and predictably ensue.

Not anymore! I thought. And with Machiavelli's maxims on setting strict limits in mind, I waged a pragmatic and proactive plan of attack. Instead of waiting for disaster to strike, I preemptively stopped the kids at the entrance and handed each of them a ten-dollar bill.

"What's this?" Teddy suspiciously asked.

"It's a ten-dollar bill," I said, stating the obvious.

"I know *that*," she said. "But what's it for?"

"It's for you to use today," I calmly explained. "But that's *all* you're gonna get, so use it wisely."

She got quiet for a while, then carefully folded the bill and tucked it in her pocket.

"What do you say?" I asked, gently but firmly.

"Huh?" she mumbled.

"What do you say?" I repeated.

She looked at me with a strange expression on her face, then smiled slightly and said, "Thanks, Mom."

"You're very welcome," I replied.

Once inside, my troops carefully examined the price of each item they liked, then made a very considered decision.

"*What??* Twenty-nine dollars?!" Teddy protested as she examined the price of a Justin Bieber backpack.

I just watched her and did not respond.

"Well, that's just ridiculous," she mumbled with disgust as she put the backpack back on the shelf. "It's not worth *that* much!"

I just smiled as we moved on.

And here's the best part of all: our shopping trip was much smoother, my kids were more appreciative, and I saved a lot of cash. Equally important, they learned the value of money as they saw how much things cost—and all because I took parenting advice from Machiavelli!

And as a strange sense of peace and well-being rose up inside of me, I thought, Hypothesis tested, and proven correct! Bring it on!!

It was a small victory. But it gave me confidence. So, more and more over the next weeks and months, I took my cue from Machiavelli whenever I faced a parenting dilemma. And the crazy part: it kept working. That's the tale I'll tell you about in the pages that follow.

But even as I applied my Machiavellian plan to my kids, and even as they started behaving better and my stress level plummeted, a small part of me was still skeptical. Did I really want to take parenting advice from a guy whose name is synonymous with morally questionable, self-serving behavior? Don't his rules seem, well, harsh? And could my kids really be happy being lorded over by a tyrannical mom?

In the end, I was more desperate than skeptical, and I kept implementing his advice, using Machiavelli's guidebook for statecraft as a manifesto for raising my family. My method: I would carefully apply his rules, one by one, to my kids and observe the results.

And while you might think that using Machiavelli to manipulate your kids into behaving better sounds sneaky or scheming, here's the thing I learned throughout the course of this enlightening, maddening, and ultimately (I think) successful journey: you can get more out of your kids, with less fight, if you gently influence them to get what you want (and let them think it's their own idea).

If this is true, then the ends *do* justify the means, especially if the "end" is having a happy, strife-free family — and a happy, stress-free mom, right? The experiment was about to start in earnest. And before too long, things stopped being so nice and tidy and started to get real.

IV

The Two Most Essential Foundations for Any Family Are Sound Rules and Strong Disciplinary Forces:
Laying Down the Law

The two most essential foundations for any state," Machiavelli proclaims, "are sound laws and strong military forces." Similarly, I reasoned by analogy, the two most essential foundations for any family are sound *rules* and strong *disciplinary* forces.

Yes! I thought. That's just what my family needs—clear rules, and then some strict discipline to enforce them.

First: the rules. One morning, not long after I secretly hatched my Machiavellian plan, I told my kids at breakfast that I would be convening our first "Family Meeting" that evening to lay down some new family rules. I knew that a diatribe on Machiavelli wasn't going to win them over. So to get them on board, I simply told them that their dad and

I, as the leaders of our family, would be setting the cardinal rules. These rules would be absolute, and they would be firmly enforced. But the good news was that the kids could suggest some rules of their own.

This was met with blank stares . . . and soon the bickering and whining resumed as if I hadn't said anything at all.

"I don't *want* waffles!" Teddy pouted. "I *want* pancakes!"

"We don't have pancakes," I said.

"Oh, yes we do," she said, pulling a box of pancake mix from the cupboard.

I sighed as I reached for the griddle, then tossed two Hot Pockets in lunch boxes, at which point Daniel grimaced and whispered, "My mom always let me buy lunch."

Eric nodded and reached in his pocket, which prompted Teddy to say, "I don't want a Hot Pocket. Can I have Pizza Rolls instead? But sausage, not pep—"

"*No!*" I hollered. "Everyone! Just *stop*!!"

They all froze. Finally they were listening to me.

"All right," I calmly announced. "We're holding our first meeting tonight—"

"Mom!" Teddy shrieked. "Katie's drawing on the wall with your lipstick!"

"Katie!" I shouted as Trevor spilled milk on the ground and began crying.

And as I reached for the sponge, I sighed and mumbled, ". . . at seven o'clock sharp."

⚜

Yes, things were off to a rocky start. But that was par for the course. So I held firm, and when we gathered around the dining-room table that night, I came armed with a large white poster board and a permanent black ink Sharpie pen.

"Okay," I began, "I'm going to write each rule on a list so you know exactly what they are, which will make it easy for you to always follow them. Make sense?"

"Yeah," Teddy said as she shrugged.

"Good!" I said, as her siblings nodded nervously in agreement.

Like most parents, I want my kids to be honest. And while Machiavelli advises that a ruler must be deceitful if it is to his advantage (more on this later), what I learned is that despite his bad rap, he was actually quite an honest and upright guy. And while he did have some major flaws (as we all do), he was a loving father, loyal friend, and brutally honest observer of human behavior. He commented on everything he saw—the cruelty, brutality, lies, and deceit—and wasn't afraid to tell it like it was.

With this example and my own commitment to the truth in mind, the first family rule I firmly established was "NO LYING."

"Everyone knows what this means, right?" I asked as I wrote the rule on the List.

More nods.

"Excellent!" I said. "Then you will all always be honest and no one will ever lie, right?"

"Right," they quietly replied.

Next on my list of cardinal sins for kids is disrespect. Now, while Machiavelli obviously didn't have young kids in mind when he penned *The Prince*, he explicitly cautions throughout his book that a leader must maintain the respect of the people. Armed with this advice, I wrote, "NO TALKING BACK" as Rule Number Two on the List.

"Do you know why this is so important?" Eric asked.

This was met with a long, knowing silence.

"Because talking back is bad," Daniel finally offered.

"Yes!" I said. "But *why* is it bad?"

"Because . . . it's not respectful," Teddy guessed.

"Yes!" I said excitedly. "That's right!"

And as her lips turned up in a proud little smile, I remembered Machiavelli's maxim that "he who wishes to be obeyed must know how to command." So the next rule I laid down was "YOU MUST ALWAYS LISTEN AND OBEY."

"All right?" I asked, scanning my angels' sweet, innocent faces.

"All right," they sighed.

"Great!" I exclaimed. Then I laid down a few more rules, like no bickering, whining, shrieking, fighting, or taking other people's things without asking.

With these ground rules established, I opened the floor for other suggestions. This was an important part of my plan—perhaps the most important of all—because I knew that I could get more out of my kids with less resistance if they thought the Rule List was partly their idea. Why? Because they'd feel a sense of ownership—and maybe even pride—in knowing they'd helped create it. In other words, if kids think they're the lawgivers, too, then they're more likely to fall into line.

"So, what else?" I asked, looking at Teddy.

"No slamming doors?" she cautiously offered.

"Excellent! Daniel?"

"No stealing," he said.

"Yes!! What else?"

"No throwing balls in the house!" Teddy shouted.

"No shouting in the house!" Daniel countered.

"No cheating in handball!"

"No tattling!"

"Yes!! Yes!!!" I said. "Now see? Isn't this FUN?!"

They nodded and kept throwing out suggestions, competing with each other to see who could come up with more rules.

After they ran out of ideas, it was time to establish my disciplinary forces. So I asked them what punishments they thought would be fair if they broke a particular rule. Taking my cue from Machiavelli's admonishment that a leader "must maintain the support of his subjects," I asked my kids to help me create a list of consequences for the violation of each rule.

"Now, what should happen if someone takes someone else's belongings without asking?"

"They'll get a time-out!" Teddy said decisively.

"Okay, for how long?"

"Uh . . . ten minutes," she said.

"How about thirty?" I suggested.

"Okay," she sighed with a look of slight fear in her eyes.

Next, I turned to Daniel, who had a bad habit of slamming his bedroom door whenever he was frustrated or angry. He knew he wasn't supposed to do this, but other than being briefly lectured by his father, no other punishments ever followed.

Remembering Machiavelli's maxim that a ruler should punish wrongdoers swiftly and severely, I suggested that if he slammed his door again, we would immediately remove it from its hinges and store it in our garage for a year.

"Sound fair?" I asked.

Daniel nodded and laughed. I don't know exactly why he laughed because I didn't ask. But I assumed then, as I do today, that it was because he thought the punishment was so extreme as to be silly, and because he was relieved to finally have some clear boundaries set in this strange new world order he was now part of.

And therein lies the beauty and Machiavellian logic of establishing sound rules and strong disciplinary forces in our home: it not only empowers Eric and me as parents, it empowers our children, too, and helps them feel more confident and in control of their lives.

"If I don't ever do X," they reason, "then Mommy and Daddy won't ever do Y."

But what happens when your kids do X (whatever X may be), as all kids inevitably do? On this, I remembered that in *The Prince* Machiavelli sets out to answer the question "How best can a ruler maintain control of his state?" In answering that question he says that a successful prince is "one who can meet any enemy on the battlefield" and "is armed with his own arms."

Okay, so this language might sound a bit harsh at first. But here's the key: in applying his rules in my life, I construe the "enemy" that I meet on the battlefield not as my kids but rather as the undesirable behaviors they occasionally exhibit—and I consider my "arms" to be that list of specific rules and punishments we agreed upon that night, which hung prominently on our refrigerator door.

These rules (and the consequences if broken) would be my main source, my touchstone, of parental happiness, power, and success. And they were another critical part of my strategy. Because only through the application of power, Machiavelli insists, can individuals (or kids) be brought to obey. And only through applying power will a ruler (or parent) be able to maintain a state (or family) in safety and security. But Machiavelli goes further. Arguing that "good laws follow from good arms," he asserts that the very legitimacy of law rests entirely upon the threat of coercive force. In other words, if you're not afraid of punishment, you're not as likely to obey the rules, right?

And as I thought about this, it hit me: young kids don't obey household rules because they love their mommy and daddy. Sure they love us. (And we adore them. Most of the time.) But they become more obedient little people because of their fear of being punished by their parents. So, if I wanted to assert my authority as a parent, I had to establish, through the threat of coercive force, my power to enforce it.

Bottom line: when it comes to princely and parental

success, it's all about power and authority, cause and effect, discipline and respect.

Now, I'm no shrinking violet when it comes to disciplining my kids. But I admit to pausing a bit when considering this Machiavellian concept. I mean, the "threat of coercive force" just sounds so militaristic, and it raises the socially explosive issue of corporal punishment, or, more precisely, in the case of parenting, the practice and act of spanking.

I should make it clear here that I do not, as a general rule, believe in spanking a child of any age. I have never spanked Teddy. I have never spanked Trevor. I have never spanked my husband (but that's an entirely different issue). And until I reached my wits' end with Katie, I had never considered spanking her. I'm not making a moral judgment. I'm simply saying that I view this particular form of discipline—good arms, as Machiavelli would say—as a parental weapon of last resort.

As fate would have it, this issue came into play when Katie tried to escape like Houdini from our house one day when she thought I wasn't watching. This was troubling enough as it was. But it wasn't a rule I'd explicitly laid out on the List. And, to be honest, in that moment when I couldn't find her, I was more scared than mad. I wasn't thinking about Machiavelli's rules. I wasn't even thinking about enforcing "good arms." I was just a protective and slightly panicky mom trying to keep her child from engaging in dangerous behavior. So, out of this primal fear and frustration, I gave her a quick pat on the behind.

Yes, I confess: I spanked my child.

Katie's eyes opened wide with surprise, but she didn't

let out so much as a whimper or whine, much less a cry. It seemed like all was forgotten, until, sure enough, she tried to pull the same trick the next day. This time, I deliberately (as opposed to emotionally) gave her another quick pat, which was met with a slight grimace . . . followed by a wide, defiant grin.

Clearly, this disciplinary strategy wasn't only ineffective, it was aggravating the situation. Or, as Francis Bacon (one of Machiavelli's earliest and biggest fans, by the way) would say, the remedy was worse than the disease.

Defeated but determined, I wondered if maybe the problem wasn't with Machiavelli's advice but with my application of it. So I scoured my old copy of *The Prince* and stumbled upon a related concept: "laws will only be obeyed if they are understood." Which makes sense, of course, but I felt like I'd laid down the law with clear and intelligible communication. I mean, what part of "DO NOT GO OUT OF THE HOUSE WITHOUT DADDY OR ME!" isn't clear or intelligible?

As I thought about this over the next few days, I realized that it wasn't the rule that was unclear. It was the punishment that was confusing to Katie. I mean, what, from her perspective, does running outside have to do with spanking? The answer: nothing. So maybe I'd picked the wrong weapon for the battle.

A few days later, Katie snuck outside again and tried to hide in the backyard. This time, I calmly followed her, then sat her down in her room and looked right in her eyes.

"You know you're not supposed to leave the house without asking, right?" I said softly but sternly.

She nodded in acknowledgment, looking shocked and confused at her mommy's newfound calmness and confidence.

"Okay, then," I announced. "You're getting a half-hour time-out in your room."

And the look on her sweet little guilt-ridden face was one of total terror and submission. "No," she whimpered as I headed for the door.

"Sorry, Katie," I said firmly. "You know the rules. And from now on, whenever you choose to break one of them, this is what I will choose to do. Every. Single. Time."

Then I slowly closed the door and walked away. And as tough as that was on both of us, it nevertheless was effective because I can honestly say that that was the first time I had ever heard her cry in the face of my discipline. But hers weren't cries of sadness or frustration. They were cries of trepidation (A *half-hour* time-out?! *Ouch!!*) and recognition (Maybe I shouldn't do that again).

That might seem extreme, especially if you're not familiar with the unique challenges of disciplining a special-needs child. I understand that. It's a very delicate and difficult issue. And I realize that I might be severely criticized for my actions and decisions in this particular instance. But when it comes to parenting and politics, context is everything. And if that kind of pragmatic and tough-minded Machiavellian strategy was what it was going to take to keep my very sweet and spirited but stubborn young daughter safe and sound, then, in my mind, at least, it was in her best interest. I felt that, in this case, the ends really *did* justify the means.

Simply talking with her didn't work. A light spank, thankfully, didn't work. But a lengthy and immediate time-out did, probably because when I firmly laid down the law, as Machiavelli admonishes, she saw that what she thought was a fun game to play with her mommy elicited not laughter but a long, boring trip to her room, and she wisely decided to fall in line. In other words, I wasn't going to abide by her rules. She was going to abide by mine. And that holds true for all of my kids.

When I walked into her room a half hour later, she was sitting on her bed flipping through a picture book. She ignored me for a while, and when she finally looked up, she stared me square in the eye and sheepishly smiled.

"You ready to come out now and behave?" I asked.

"Yah!" she said, then giggled and clapped.

And with that victory scored, I took a deep sigh of relief and walked her calmly out of the room, confident in the knowledge that Machiavelli's rules could help me gently influence her—and all my kids—to be better behaved.

Remember: a Machiavellian approach to parenting is all about power, authority, discipline, and respect, with a healthy dose of fear and self-interested cause and effect thrown in. And the best part of all: my kids now know our rules because they helped create them. And they know exactly what will happen if they break them—which is why they choose to obey them. Mostly. (More on that later.)

Most important, they know that they have a very strong and strict but fair mom who loves them very much. But as Machiavelli explicitly cautions throughout his book, it's not enough for a leader to simply acquire power. Power must be maintained, a task that is often fraught with great conflict and danger—for a prince and for a parent.

V

It Is More Difficult to Rule a New Principality Than a Hereditary One: On Disciplining Stepchildren

So, I established (at least for the moment) sound rules and strong disciplinary forces in my home—now what? Not sure of my next move, I grabbed my copy of *The Prince* and noticed that Machiavelli begins it by classifying the various types of governments into two basic types: republics and principalities (so called because they're ruled by a "prince" or single leader). He then describes all principalities as either hereditary, in which a prince has been long established, or new, such as new territories that have been "conquered by force or acquired through fortune or virtù" (more on these central terms later).

Building on these observations, Machiavelli says that

fewer difficulties arise for a prince in a hereditary state because his subjects are familiar with him and accustomed to his rule. Moreover, their natural inclination is to love the prince and his family, unless some terrible offense is committed. But when a prince (or a parent) acquires a new principality and attempts to rule over their new subjects, disaster often ensues.

At least it did for me.

Not long after Eric and I tied the knot, one of the greatest difficulties I faced involved the disciplining of my new "subject," Daniel—my sweet, kind, and stubborn then-six-year-old stepson—who was acting out (read: rebelling) a lot. Most of it was typical kid stuff, like talking back to his dad and throwing tantrums when he didn't get that new Webkinz puppy or kitten that he so desperately wanted and needed.

As he grew older, however, he began engaging in more troubling behavior, like lying to get out of trouble ("I swear I didn't eat that last cookie," he would say with crumbs on his face), cheating in otherwise friendly handball games (*"Footsie!"* he'd shout as Teddy frowned and looked down at her tiny little feet, which were clearly in bounds), and occasionally pocketing spare change that wasn't his.

Lying, cheating, and "stealing" are cardinal sins in my parental book, as they are for Eric. But my husband had only one overnight each week with Daniel, and the last thing he wanted to do was spend that time cracking down on him. And so, not long after I hatched my Machiavellian plan, Eric asked me to help him out in the Discipline Department.

Armed with my copy of *The Prince*, I readily enlisted in this battle. And whenever Daniel would break a family rule, I would discipline him just as swiftly and severely as I would were any of the other kids to engage in similar behavior. As you can imagine, this was not so well received.

Things came to a head one Saturday afternoon when I saw Daniel pick up a crumpled one-dollar bill that must've fallen out of my wallet. I watched him look around, then quietly slip it in his pocket. Like some parents might do, I immediately construed this as a deliberate and intentional act of "stealing"—behavior that was explicitly prohibited on the List.

Would Daniel come clean? I hoped so. But I didn't know. So I approached him like a cunning Machiavellian cop confronting a petty bandit or thief.

"Hey, Daniel?" I casually asked. "Did you happen to see a one-dollar bill? It was on the floor a few minutes ago but now it's not here."

He looked at me and guiltily shook his head no.

Now the stakes were even higher because not only had he swiped something that wasn't his, he was fibbing about it. Maintaining my composure, I gave him another chance to fess up. "You *sure*?" I said firmly. "Because I *know* it was just here."

Another guilty shake of the head was his only response.

At that point, Eric came downstairs, so I pulled him aside and quietly briefed him on the situation. He, too, was concerned.

"Hey, buddy," he said. "Did you find a dollar bill in here?"

"Uh . . . no," Daniel said, looking right into his dad's eyes. And at that point I had had enough.

"Yes," I said firmly. "I saw him pick it up and put it in his pocket."

Daniel just stood there, his expression now frozen with fear.

Wanting to protect his young son, Eric shot me a look like I was a renegade cop who was overreacting. Still, I held firm and calmly asked Daniel to empty his pocket—out of which, of course, spilled the crumpled one-dollar bill.

Aha! A great learning moment! I thought as I reprimanded him. But, of course, this incident didn't go over so well with Daniel, and it quickly became clear that my new stepson wasn't particularly fond of me.

As instructive as this incident was, it was also somewhat uncomfortable and tense, especially since Eric thought I was disciplining Daniel more harshly than the other kids, and I felt like I had been thrown under the proverbial bus as a parent. But instead of getting worked up and taking it personally, I took a deep breath and turned to Machiavelli in hopes of finding a strategy to help me resolve this intractable and seemingly unwinnable battle. As strange as it sounds, I found guidance in his insights on the difficulties of governing a new principality.

In particular, Machiavelli says that "when states are acquired in a country differing in language, customs, or laws, there are difficulties, and good fortune and great energy are needed to hold them." Tell me about it. But, reasoning rather broadly and loosely by analogy, it hit me that the difficulties that Daniel was struggling with as a new stepson stemmed partly from the fact that he was accustomed to differing family customs and rules at his mother's house.

Yet aside from trying to maintain as much continuity in his life as possible (similar manners and rules, etc.), there wasn't too much I could do to change that fact. So what is a new prince (or stepparent) to do?

Like the Shell Answer Man, Machiavelli always has a helpful tip to offer, and here he says that "one of the greatest and most real helps would be that he who has acquired a new state should go and reside there."

Go and reside there? Okay. I was not, for obvious logistical reasons, going to go and reside at the house that Daniel shares with his mom. That, I'm fairly certain, would be ill-advised. But what I could and did do was use Machiavelli's insights on new principalities to view my relationship with Daniel in an objective new light.

And it helped. Because once I looked at this battle from his perspective instead of mine, I was able to see that the difficulties that he was facing as a new stepson—and that many new stepchildren must inevitably confront—arose from an inherent difficulty that exists in all blended families. Unlike a hereditary family wherein a ruler is a child's own biological mother or father whom he naturally trusts and loves, a ruler in a new principality (or newly blended family) is unfamiliar to the subject and must earn his trust and love.

Clearly, I had some work to do.

⚜

Here again, Machiavelli has useful advice to offer. This time, it was his tip that "subjects in new principalities change their rulers willingly." What does this have to do with parenting? Well, Daniel obviously didn't choose me willingly, and I was fairly certain that he'd ditch me in a minute if he had the chance—especially after I called him out on the missing one-dollar bill.

And as I thought about this, it hit me that maybe we couldn't change his rulers (his mom, Eric, and me) but we could change who ended up enforcing the laws. In other words, if I were in Daniel's shoes, I'd rather be disciplined by Eric than by me. That's not to say that I was willing or thought it wise to totally abdicate my authority as a stepparent. But I did think that it was in Daniel's best interest, and the best interest of our family as a whole, if Eric resumed primary control in the Disciplining-of-Daniel Department.

Not long after this partial transfer of power, Daniel decided it might be fun to throw one of Teddy's stuffed animals into the spinning blades of the old ceiling fan in her room. I didn't actually witness this trick. I just happened to stumble upon its aftermath when I entered the room and saw a broken blade lying on the edge of Teddy's bed.

"What happened?" I asked.

No answer.

"What *happened*?" I asked again, looking at Teddy.

Not wanting to rat Daniel out, she shrugged and looked down at the ground.

"You have to tell me what happened, Teddy," I said sternly. "Someone could've gotten really hurt if they were hit by that blade."

She looked up reluctantly and whispered, "Daniel threw my bear in the fan."

"You threw the bear in the fan when it was spinning?" I said incredulously to him.

"Yeah," he said with a nervous laugh. "It's a game. But it wasn't supposed to break."

Now, what I wanted to say right then and there was "You've gotta be kidding me? Not only was that really dumb. It was really dangerous," which of course was the truth of the matter. But channeling Machiavelli's insights on new principalities gave me the objectivity to view this situation from Daniel's perspective instead of mine. (I mean, I could see how kids might think this particular "trick" was kind of amusing.) Equally important, it gave me the restraint not to overreact or emotionally respond. Instead, I calmly conferred with Eric and he took control of the situation.

"You know that was a stupid thing to do, Daniel," he said as he tried to fix the fan.

"Yeah," Daniel nodded.

"And you know it was dangerous?"

"I didn't know it would break," he replied in his own defense.

"I know you didn't," Eric said. "But you have to promise us that you'll never do that again. Promise?"

"Yes," Daniel nodded. "I promise."

Aha! I thought. A great learning moment at last!

And here's the best part of all: instead of throwing a hissy fit whenever an offense is committed, I just kick back, zip my trap, and watch the discipline go down from a safe, neutral distance. Think Switzerland. It's a win-win situation. That's what we're after.

Bottom line: before I began reading *The Prince*, I would take my stepson's misbehavior personally, his defiance as a symbol of how he didn't respect me. But applying Machiavelli's insights to my life gave me the clarity to consider our relationship more objectively and I stopped blaming him for occasionally misbehaving, as all kids naturally do. And that one simple shift made a significant difference for all of us as our home front, which had once resembled a battlefield torn by warring factions, became more peaceful and stable.

And if you're a stepparent, or even if you're not, a sense of peace and predictability brought on by stability is always a winning strategy. The key is not to overreact or take things personally when problems arise. Yes, it's easy for a parent to take a child's misbehavior personally. But here's what I learned from Machiavelli on this: when family conflicts, battles, or disasters strike—and they will—always try to assess the situation calmly and from an objective perspective. If *you* can behave this way, then your home life *will* become more peaceful and stable—and, as an added bonus, your blood pressure will quickly plummet, just like mine did!

And with this victory scored, I took a deep sigh of relief and set my sights on an entirely different parental battle altogether.

VI

It Is of Great Importance That a Child in the Tender Years of His Youth Hears Any Act Praised or Censured: The Power of Positive Reinforcement

I wanted my daughter Teddy to read more, especially since I could vividly remember how much reading had enriched my life as a child. Lots of moms want this for their kids, right? But despite my begging, pleading, wheedling, and conniving to get my intelligent little seven-year-old to pick up a book that wasn't assigned homework, she would much rather watch TV or ride her bike than spend quality time curled up with a Dr. Seuss book.

But could *The Prince* help me win this battle? I wasn't sure. So I turned first to Machiavelli's personal letters for some insight into the man, and what I learned was that he was a devoted father who cared deeply for his family. What I also learned was that one of his greatest parental desires was that his children occupy the "tender years of their youth" in a continual pursuit of knowledge, not only for its own sake but for the ways in which it would invariably contribute to the betterment of their lives.

Yes! I thought. That's what all parents want!

And as I kept reading, I stumbled upon a letter that Machiavelli wrote to his son Guido on this very issue. "I have received your letter," Niccolò wrote, "which has given me the greatest pleasure, especially because you tell me you are quite restored in health, than which I could have no better news; for if God grant life to you, and to me, I hope to make a good man of you if you are willing to do your share." Then, referring to his son's new patron, he added, "This will turn out well for you, but it is necessary for you to study; and since you have no longer the excuse of illness, take pains to study letters and music, for you see what honor is done to me for the little skill I have. Therefore, my son, if you wish to please me, and to bring success and honor to yourself, do right and study, because others will help you if you help yourself."

Five centuries later in Southern California, my own father was encouraging my older brother, Mark, and me to do the same, and one of my fondest childhood memories is of our biweekly pilgrimages to our neighborhood library. We would go in the early evenings after we had finished our homework. Once we got there, Dad (like Draco) would lay down the law regarding how many books we could select, but what we chose was our own domain.

And, just like that, I fell madly in love.

Miss Suzy and her abandoned toy soldiers captured my

heart first, followed by the high adventures of *Little House on the Prairie; The Lion, the Witch, and the Wardrobe;* and *A Wrinkle in Time.* After that, I fell fast and hard for Peter Pan, the boy who could magically fly and never grow up (imagine that!), the rambunctious and fun-loving young Wilbur (to this day, I still fall in love with the runt), and the wacky but wise Willy Wonka (Gene Wilder would later become my first major movie-star crush, only to be rivaled by Bobby Brady, Steve Martin, and George Clooney—call me!!). My favorite of all might have been *Alice in Wonderland* and that charming if ever-irascible Cheshire Cat, whose habit of gradually disappearing (leaving behind only his grin) made me think—imagine that!—all over again.

And on the way to and from those regular trips to the library, my father would often pepper me with questions to gauge my progress and comprehension. So how did Miss Suzy get back her cozy little home in that old oak tree? What happened to Augustus Gloop and Mike Teevee? And where did that magical wardrobe lead? All the while, he would praise me for what a good reader I was.

And that's the thing about reading. Just as we can lead a proverbial horse to water but can't make it drink, we can lead our kids to the library but can't make them read. Or at least, we can't make them love it.

That must come from within.

To my delight, Teddy took an interest in reading from an early age, and during the summer between kindergarten and first grade, she read one hundred picture books, from *Chicka Chicka Boom Boom* and *Click Clack Moo* to *Where the Wild Things Are* and *Goodnight Moon.* With the encouragement of her father, who brilliantly spearheaded and supervised the project, she wrote the title of each book she had read on a list, taking great pride at her progress as her list grew ever longer.

Equally important, she seemed to really enjoy reading—until second grade, at which point her engagement with books swiftly dwindled to nil. So, to get her to read more, I did what many other moms might well meaningly but misguidedly do: I resorted to bribery.

"If you read *Island of the Blue Dolphins* or *Tiger Beat* magazine for a half hour," I'd strategically offer like Johnnie Cochran, "then I'll take you to Baskin-Robbins."

"All right," she'd say with a sigh as she rolled her eyes, then sit down and begrudgingly do it.

Anything for a Strawberry Fruit Blast, right?

Fearing that time was quickly slipping by and that she might not ever develop a love of reading, I turned to Machiavelli in hopes of finding a strategy to help me reverse this disturbing trend. This time I read a maxim that became another directly helpful rule on the List: "It is of great importance that a child in the tender years of his youth hears any act praised or censured, for this necessarily makes a lasting impression upon his mind and becomes afterwards the rule of his life for all time."

No sooner did I see this gem than I realized that I had been taking the wrong approach. And by that I mean that my acts of bribery could be construed as a subtle form of "censure." Perhaps I was inadvertently but dangerously equating reading with some form of a chore, a boring but necessary means to a more exciting and pleasurable end.

And, as Machiavelli would admonish, this type of censure, this negative message I was sending about reading, could make a lasting impression on her mind and become the rule of her life for all time.

What I needed, then, was a paradigm shift and quick. So instead of bribing her with ice cream, I instead began lavishly praising her and engaging her whenever she read for pleasure.

"So you like *The Dumb Bunnies*?" I asked one day as she played yet another Angry Birds game on my iPhone.

"Yeah, it's pretty funny," she said without taking her eyes off the screen.

"What's it about?"

She looked at me and grinned when the game ended. "It's about this family of bunnies that does the opposite of what you're supposed to."

"Really?" I asked. "Like what?"

"Like, when it's raining they go to the beach," she said as she laughed, "or have a picnic at the car wash."

I laughed with her, then asked, "Wanna read it to me?"

She looked at me with a strange expression on her face, then put down my iPhone and grabbed the book from the table.

"Let's see," she said. She turned to the first page and began reading, hesitantly at first, then with increasing playfulness and animation.

This victory proved fleeting, however, and in the days and weeks that passed, she rarely opened a book other than to do her homework. Feeling defeated, I let my thoughts turn again to Machiavelli, who, as we have seen, actively encouraged his own kids to read. But why, I wondered, did *he* become such a bibliophile?

Was it by nature or nurture?

Curious, I did a little research, and what I learned is that his own book-loving father encouraged him to read as a young child. Bernardo Machiavelli was a respected but by no means wealthy Florentine lawyer. His most notable trait, other than being perpetually in debt, was his passion for books, and he had at "considerable expense" assembled "a small personal library" that included books by Aristotle, Cicero, and other Greek and Roman philosophers, works by the great masters of rhetoric, and volumes of Italian history—some of which he borrowed or rented with the fruits of his labor on his modest family farm in the rolling, vineyard-covered hills just south of Florence. (This was the same farm, by the way, that Niccolò would later inherit and where he would later pen *The Prince*).

In any event, to get his hands on an upcoming edition of Livy's *History of Rome*, Bernardo agreed to compile an index of place-names in it for a Florentine publisher. "The task was exacting and dull and took nine months," historian Sebastian De Grazia notes, "but in exchange he was allowed to keep the book." And so it was that his son was able to read and reread at his leisure Livy's account of "the political and military achievements that transformed a small city into a free, powerful republic."

Machiavelli's first taste of politics, then, and his passion for books came from the encouragement and patient labor of his father.

What a valuable gift for a parent to give to a child,

right? I mean, had Bernardo been a merchant or banker and sent his impressionable young son off to work in Florence each day instead of immersing him in the world of books, Machiavelli might not have written *The Prince* or gone on to become Italy's greatest writer of prose.

With this in mind, I decided to step up my efforts by writing and publishing my own little books to suit Teddy's interests. Like many kids, she's a great animal lover, so I quickly penned a picture book called *The Day Abraham Lincoln Saved Three Little Kittens* and then one about Teddy Roosevelt and the invention of the teddy bear. After that, I got a bit more ambitious and wrote a chapter book about seven-year-old twins who travel back in time to solve a series of historical riddles and then one about a ten-year-old girl named Zoey Zoolander who adopts a stray cat and teaches it to perform all kinds of strange and amazing tricks. And, to my delight, Teddy gobbled them up faster than I could write them. But this pattern abruptly ground to a halt when she entered third grade.

Oh well, I thought, maybe she's just not a reader. And I slowly and silently tried to come to peace with that.

Then one day after picking her up from school, I sat at my laptop as she prepared an afternoon snack. Not more than two or three minutes had passed when she looked up at me and asked, "I'm *so* bored, Mom. Can we go to Baskin-Robbins?"

"Sorry, honey," I said with a shrug. "I have to work."

She sighed, then headed for the stairs with her Pizza Rolls. But after a half hour or so, I realized that our house was unusually, almost eerily quiet. No *iCarly* blasting from the TV. No Angry Birds chirping from my iPhone screen. And, as I headed for the stairs, my heart suddenly skipped a beat because I saw her sitting there with my new Kindle wedged tightly between her greasy little fingers.

"Look, Mom!" she said. "It's Zoey Zoolander!"

"You're right," I said and nodded. "But didn't you already read that?"

"Yeah," she whispered, "but I wanna read it again."

"That's great, honey," I praised her and then just smiled and walked away.

Once again, Machiavelli had helped me see the errors of my ways. In particular, his insights on censuring a child helped me realize, however ironically, that my attempt to manipulate my daughter into reading more was not only ineffective but ill-advised. Equally important, his advice on praising a child helped me see that I didn't need to take extraordinary measures like writing my own children's books to pique Teddy's interest in reading.

I just needed to relax a bit, and try to always praise her and engage her whenever she read for pleasure—even *Captain Underpants and the Perilous Plot of Professor Poopypants* or the back of a Frosted Flakes box, for that matter. To add to the fun, we now take frequent trips to our neighborhood bookstore, and I recently gave her my old Kindle with dozens of digital books on it. I'm not sure if she'll ever be as fervent a reader or writer as I am. But I guess all I can hope for is that my love of reading, and our time reading together, will make a lasting impression on her mind. And maybe, just maybe, it will ignite a passion for reading that will become a "rule" of her life for all time.

Bottom line: to influence your child's behavior, don't censure, criticize, bribe, or blame—because that simply diminishes your power and creates more resistance, anger, resentment, and shame. Instead, wait for them to display good behavior and then lavishly praise and engage.

Think Pavlov's dogs. It's all about conditioning. And I'm convinced that Machiavelli would agree with me on this.

VII

A Prince Ought to Study the Actions of Illustrious Men:
Teaching by Example

With the school year quickly coming to an end, I began brainstorming ways to keep my kids entertained during the long, hot dog days of summer. This wasn't necessarily a problem that I would have thought to turn to Machiavelli with, but it turns out he has a few words of advice that can help out here, too.

Machiavelli was all about learning from the past. In fact, he backs up his many edicts in *The Prince* with an astonishingly wide array of historical examples, from classical antiquity to Renaissance Italy. He even advises that the study of history can do much to enrich the mind. This, for him, was an important "end" in itself. But he also believed that a deep knowledge of history could be used as a means to help a ruler become a great leader. This is so important that it became the next rule on our List.

In particular, he writes that "to enrich the intellect, men ought to read histories and study there the actions of illustrious men to see how they have borne themselves in war, to examine the causes of their victories and defeat, so as to avoid the latter and imitate the former."

Study history? I thought. This one I've got covered!

And by that I mean that even though I received a law degree and passed the California State Bar before I had kids, my "true love"—professionally and intellectually speaking—is and always has been history, so much so that I worked toward and earned my PhD in history in the spring of 2008, after many long (but happy and rewarding!) years of study. Needless to say, I was thrilled with Machiavelli's advice and I decided to share my enthusiasm for history with my kids by teaching them a bit about the American presidents.

Like many parents and teachers might do, I first tried to encourage them to memorize the names of each president in chronological order. Fun, right? But for some reason their attention kept drifting off well before we even made our way to Abraham Lincoln.

"John Quincy who?" Teddy asked.

"Adams," I repeated.

"Oh, yeah," she yawned. "Can I have another Popsicle?"

Of course, simply memorizing names and dates isn't the point of history anyway. It's all about the stories, some of which, as in the case of Richard Nixon, for instance, prove the adage that the truth sometimes really is stranger than fiction. I mean, Watergate plumbers, wiretaps, and the Saturday Night Massacre? No one would believe that unless it actually happened, right?

So, to spice things up, I did a little culinary detective work and began sharing fun anecdotes and facts about the presidents' favorite foods. Once I dug up the recipes and we talked about the presidents who might have eaten them, I'd take a stab at preparing the dishes, some of which, due to my incompetence in the kitchen, turned out a lot worse than others.

"George Washington Hoe Cakes? Yuck!"

"Andrew Jackson Benne Wafers? No thanks!"

"Richard Nixon Family-Style Meat Loaf? Ugh! Not *again*!!"

Nevertheless, I continued on my quest and eventually turned those stories and recipes into a food history blog for parents and kids. Soon, it started getting some nice attention, and my kids were home with me one day when I was being interviewed about the blog for a feature story in our local newspaper.

"So, how was the Harry Truman Tuna Noodle Casserole?" the reporter bitingly inquired.

"Ugh," Teddy said, scrunching up her face. "It was *disgusting*!"

Like I said, I'm not much of a cook.

But Machiavelli isn't advising a prince to study history for the sake of knowledge itself but to help him resist the disastrous malice of fate. Similarly, I wasn't teaching my kids about the presidents for the sake of knowledge itself.

My goal: to use food as a means to introduce them to the various virtues and personality traits that made each of our presidents—especially the Founding Fathers—great.

Toward that end, I spoke of George Washington's honesty, integrity, and selfless devotion to our young republic; of Thomas Jefferson's intelligence, inventiveness, and commitment to defending liberty in the face of oppression; and of John Adams and James Madison's desire to protect the rights of the people, something that, as I told my kids, found voice in their drive for the Bill of Rights, from which we all derive benefits in a multitude of ways.

"Like how?" Teddy asked one day as we made Thomas Jefferson Macaroni and Cheese while I talked to her about his many Machiavellian virtùs as a leader.

"Like, in our freedom of speech and religion."

"But we don't go to church."

"And," I added, "in our right to be free from unreasonable searches and seizures."

"But Katie always sneaks in my room and steals my stuff."

"You're right," I sighed. "But the Bill of Rights only applies to governmental interference."

"Huh?"

So much for my civics lesson.

But here's the key: just as it's not enough for a republic to have the good fortune of having a virtuous leader, it's not enough for a family to have virtuous parents. Instead, we, as parents, must instill virtue in our kids for the greater good of our families. And so it was that in teaching my kids about the presidents, I sought to instill in them the virtues of honesty, integrity, courage, and purpose, not only for the ways in which these traits will inevitably lead to the betterment of their lives, but for the greater glory and grandeur of our family.

Moving from fortune to misfortune, something that Machiavelli was all too familiar with in his own illustrious life, I applied the second half of his maxim that "a prince should study the mistakes of great men so as to avoid them" by talking to my kids about the importance of learning from their failures and mistakes.

"You struck out five times? You'll do better next time!"

"You came in last place in butterfly? Nice try!"

"You fumbled in the end zone? But I bet it was a great catch!"

To which my competitive sports-loving husband, channeling Vince Lombardi, invariably countered, "Show me a good loser and I'll show you a *loser!*"

Nice.

But mindful of the need to strike a balance between childhood coddling and competitiveness, I resolved that no one was going to interfere with my quest to instill a healthy sense of confidence, persistence, sportsmanship, and humility in my kids.

And to get my dear husband on board (read: make him pipe down), I reminded him of golfing great Bobby Jones. Renowned for his sportsmanship and sense of fair play,

Jones once said, "I never learned anything from a tournament I won." But the most famous example of his integrity came in the 1925 US Open tournament. On the final day of play, Jones insisted on calling a one-point penalty shot on himself even though no one but he had witnessed the infraction. And guess what? Yep, he lost the tournament by one stroke in a play-off. But while he lost the match, he gained universal praise for his honesty and fair play. Bothered by the adulation, Jones reportedly replied, "You might as well praise me for not robbing banks."

I'm not sure what Machiavelli would have made of Bobby Jones. But, however counterintuitive (the ends of "winning" certainly weren't justified or achieved by the means), I have a hunch that he would have praised Jones in this particular instance. Because even though he lost a tournament by practicing honesty, in the end his virtue earned him an even greater glory and prestige among the people than had he simply clinched the title.

And that, I thought, is another fabulous example of how the study of history and the actions of illustrious men can help all of us as parents to instill such virtues as honesty and integrity in our kids.

Continuing on my "history" quest, and moving from golf back to politics, I set my sights again on the Founding Fathers—and when it comes to virtue, it's tough to top George Washington. As it turns out, Washington's leadership in founding our nation and ensuring its survival points to an essential question that Machiavelli raises in *The Prince*. In particular, Machiavelli says that it's not enough that a leader be virtuous. Instead, the key to preserving liberty lies in maintaining the quality of "virtù" in the citizenry as a whole. While "virtù" sounds a lot like "virtue," the two words don't mean quite the same thing. For Machiavelli, virtù embraces boldness, bravery, foresight, flexibility, action, ingenuity, and those traits necessary for a leader to maintain a state. These same qualities, he insists, must also exist in the individual and in the citizenry as a whole if the state is not only to thrive but to survive.

The same could be said of our kids. Because not only to thrive but to survive in this world, they—like us—must also possess boldness, bravery, flexibility, and ingenuity, as well as a healthy dose of craftiness and pride, right?

This, I learned, raises a further question, the most important one of all: If we decide that we do want "virtù" as well as "virtue" in our sweet, precious, littlest subjects, then how can we instill this quality widely enough, and maintain it long enough, to ensure that civic glory is attained? In other words, how, exactly, do we keep good behavior going?

Machiavelli answers by conceding that "an element of good fortune is always involved." But he argues that no state can become great unless it is first set on the right path by a great founding father. By the same token, no family can become great unless it is first set on the right path by great parents, right? The reason we need this "first fortune," Machiavelli cautions, is that "the act of establishing a state can never be brought about through the virtù of the masses." Why? Because men are naturally greedy, hypocritical, disloyal, and deceitful, and their "diverse opinions will always prevent them from being suited to organize a government."

So our kids are going to naturally misbehave, and it's up to us to keep them in line. We don't need Machiavelli to tell us that. But here's the key: the act of establishing order in a family can never be brought about through the virtue of our kids alone, as their naturally immature, self-serving opinions will always get in their way.

But Machiavelli leaves us with a glimmer of hope. Because he says that what's needed for a state's salvation is to have a virtuous ruler "who will organize it so that its subsequent fortunes come to rest instead upon the virtù of the masses."

Okay. So the fortune of a state depends on the virtù of the people. Toward similar ends, it's our duty as parents to instill said virtù in our young subjects—our kids. And as I thought about this I remembered the famous "George Washington and the Cherry Tree" myth—the moral of which both symbolizes and celebrates the honesty of Washington as a young child. With this in mind, I dug up an old recipe for Cherry Cobbler one day and then told the story to my kids.

"So . . . George Washington's dad was mad that he cut the old cherry tree down," Teddy slowly said, "but he was happier that George told the truth?"

"Yep," I said. "Make sense?"

She nodded, then got quiet for a while. "So, if I did

something wrong," she finally asked, "I should tell you about it?"

"Yes. Always."

"And you won't get mad at me?"

"Well, I might get mad," I laughed. "But I'd be a million times more mad and disappointed if you lied about it. Honesty is one of the most important, if not the most important, virtues a person can have."

She nodded again, then whispered, "I left my jacket at school today."

"You left it at school *again*?"

"Yeah," she said softly. "Are you mad?"

"No," I laughed again. "I'm just glad you told me, but you *do* need to be more careful with your things. Okay?"

"Okay," she smiled with relief.

After we retrieved the jacket from the Lost and Found, we went home and baked a George Washington Cherry Cobbler while I talked to my kids a bit about his leadership during the Revolutionary War.

"Did you know that George Washington was the first president?" Teddy asked as she cracked an egg.

"Yep," I said, "and do you know which one was the fifth?"

She thought about it a bit. Then her eyes lit up. "John Quincy Madison!"

Close enough.

And besides, the point of history isn't memorizing names and dates anyway, right? Instead, the study of history and the actions of eminent men can do much to enrich the mind, as Machiavelli so wisely advised, and can also help a ruler become a more thoughtful and successful leader. And *that*, I thought, is yet another great tidbit of advice for all modern moms and dads.

VIII

Tardiness Often Robs Us of Opportunity and the Proper Dispatch of Forces:
Learning Not to Procrastinate

My experiment, it seemed, was succeeding. I had established sound rules and strong disciplinary forces in my home. I had ironed out some major kinks in my relationship with my stepson. Teddy was reading more. And my kids were learning about Big Ideas from the Great Men (and Women) of history. It was all thanks to Machiavelli (though no one but I knew it yet).

But there was one issue that plagued us as a family—me as well as the kids—and threatened our Machiavellian momentum. It was a chronic problem faced by countless folks, young and old . . . but one that most of us decide we can deal with tomorrow.

That problem: procrastination. This, of course, was an issue in Machiavelli's day, too—so much so that he warns his readers, in one of his most famous maxims: "A wise man does at once what a fool does finally."

He's referring here, of course, to the bad habit of putting tasks off to the future, something that in military affairs and affairs of state can be disastrous for a prince—and disastrous in family affairs for parents and kids.

Accordingly, with Teddy in second grade and Daniel third, I turned to an issue that all parents of school-age kids must inevitably confront—HOMEWORK! For some reason, their schoolwork always seemed to be put off to the last minute. If a book report was due on Monday, I'd often learn of it late Sunday night. If there was a Friday spelling test, I'd hear about it on Thursday just before bedtime. The result: stress, anxiety, and frustration.

There had to be a better way. So, six months into my experiment, I decided to take a proactive Machiavellian approach regarding homework. First, I set a firm and fast rule on *when* it must be done (before dinner). Next, I established *where* it was to be done (at the dining-room table or a desk). Finally, I laid down the law on *how* it was to be done (neatly, eagerly, TV-free, and completely).

This was met with dramatic sighs and eye rolls. But this wasn't my first rodeo. When Daniel pocketed that one-dollar bill, I channeled Machiavelli's commitment to the truth and called him on it. When Katie ran outside and tried to hide, I applied a tough-minded strategy by giving her a lengthy and immediate time-out. And when Teddy yelled in frustration at her adoring but annoying younger siblings,

I talked to her about Abraham Lincoln's virtues of kindness, compassion, and love of all creatures great and small!

So, when it came to homework, I held firm and—guess what? It worked! No more nagging, pleading, begging, bartering, threatening, harassing, or even asking. And best of all: when their new habit began paying dividends in the form of higher grades, they began to take great pride in doing it. Seriously. I wouldn't kid you about something as miraculous as that.

But it wasn't just my kids who needed to master the bad habit of procrastination. I, too, had a tendency to put off unpleasant tasks until tomorrow. Or the next day. Or, better yet, a day or two after that. Not with work—because I know that "deadlines," as a wise professor once said, "are your friends!" But when I have a difficult phone call to make or a broken dishwasher or vacuum to replace, I'm a master at finding dozens of other tasks to put on my to-do list—like, say, racing to Macy's to buy a new pair of running shoes or a few tubes of Pretty Please MAC lipstick—all of which suddenly become incredibly pressing and urgent.

To overcome these bad habits, I turned to Machiavelli. This time, I read this maxim: "Tardiness often robs us of opportunity and the proper dispatch of forces." Sounds like he's talking about war, right? But how might this apply in my life as a mom? I didn't have a clue. So I decided to think about it a bit and plot my next Machiavellian move while taking a quick mother-son walk to the park.

It was a Tuesday afternoon and I had been pushing Trevor in a swing for only a minute or two when a cute little girl skipped up to us and started talking—and by talking, I don't mean simple three- or four-word sentences that contained references to Barney or Elmo. No, hers were long, complex, perfectly articulated sentences, ones that suddenly reminded me of *Ulysses* and, if written, would've required multiple semicolons, dashes, and ellipses.

When the girl's mother finally approached, I turned to her in astonishment and said, "Wow! Your daughter talks really well. How old is she? Three? Four?"

The mother smiled wearily and, in a voice barely above a whisper, said, "She just turned two . . . and she never. Stops. Talking."

And that's when the parental panic and paranoia set in because even though Trevor was now three, he hadn't clearly said "Mommy" or "Daddy" yet, much less uttered a complete sentence. Until then, I had tried to reassure myself that every child develops at his or her own rate, especially when it comes to speech. I knew Trevor wasn't saying much, and I also knew that boys tend to develop speech a bit more slowly than girls. But if I was being brutally honest with myself, I also knew that I was stuck in denial mode as I couldn't bear the thought of two of my kids having learning disabilities. As I glanced back at that little Miss Chatty Cathy, who was still cheerfully delivering her soliloquy, and then at Trevor, who was staring blankly at the ground with his thumb in his mouth, I became increasingly worried that something might be seriously wrong with my beautiful, sweet, perfect baby boy.

Trying to act calm, I waved good-bye to the little girl and her mother, then lifted Trevor out of the swing, strapped him into his stroller, and raced frantically back to our house. Maybe he has autism! I thought, as my stomach clenched up in knots. Or maybe he has fetal alcohol syndrome because I took that sip of champagne when I was seven months pregnant with him! Or maybe he has a serious cognitive problem and won't ever talk because I didn't take him to a speech pathologist early enough!

Thankfully, he was asleep by the time we got home, so I quickly tucked him into bed and typed into Google "MY THREE-YEAR-OLD ISN'T TALKING." Immediately, dozens of relevant hits popped up. Some of the words were reassuring, especially those from moms whose once non-talking toddlers had grown out of their speech-delayed phase.

"One possible reason for delayed speech," one mother wrote, "is that you might be letting your child watch too much TV." Yes, maybe that's it, I thought, vowing to immediately get rid of our television set. "Or lack of socialization with his peers might be a cause," another mom thoughtfully posited. All right, I thought to myself and sighed, glancing at my stack of unfinished briefs. Maybe I should arrange more pool parties and playdates.

And the more I thought about it, the more the "lack of socialization" explanation made sense, because other than spending a few hours each week at our neighborhood day care center, Trevor spent most of his time playing at home with Katie.

But Katie was four at the time, and she wasn't talking either. Well, to be fair, she was talking (talking a lot, in fact), but it was her own special language she was speaking, one that was totally foreign and unintelligible to me but that Trevor had quickly picked up on. They'd sit there for hours, playing with their toys and occasionally glancing at the TV, engaging all the while in their own secret Katie-Trevor-speak.

One night, my friend Kristen came over for a glass of wine, and, after listening to them for a while, she started laughing hysterically and said, "Oh my god! They sound like Teletubbies!"

And the funny/sad/comic/tragic thing is: she was right. My kids did sound a lot like Tinky Winky and Po.

Quickly reaching for my wine, I realized that the upside was that at least they were talking, even if I had no idea what they were talking about. Still, I wasn't convinced that the cause of Trevor's delayed speech was as simple as too much TV or not enough playdates or too much time spent mimicking his sister's speech. And the more studies I read, the more I began to freak out.

One particularly alarming study indicated that a delay in speech development may be a symptom of many disorders, including hearing loss, an expressive language disorder, autism, psychosocial deprivation, and cerebral palsy. Early intervention in these types of cases is critical, experts say, because the human brain develops so rapidly in the early childhood years. If one seeks intervention too late, one risks missing an opportunity to effectively treat the problem. Or, as Machiavelli admonishes, "Tardiness often robs us of opportunity and the proper dispatch of forces."

Was I already too late? Had my inability (or unwillingness) to acknowledge a problem with my son's delayed speech done him irreparable harm?

⚜

Like much of the advice in *The Prince*, Machiavelli is referring here to military action and the proper conduct of war. Indeed, much of his book is devoted to describing exactly what it means to wage a successful war: how to effectively fortify a city, how to govern subjects in new principalities, and how to prevent domestic insurrections that might threaten a prince's rule.

Still, I didn't know how these concepts might apply to my concerns about my own son's speech delay until I thought again about Machiavelli's concept of virtù. Remember that from before? Virtù, for Machiavelli, is an essential quality, the touchstone of political and military success. In particular, the concept entails "the idea of tremendous inner fortitude to overcome even the most recalcitrant opposition" and embraces such traits as boldness, bravery, ingenuity, flexibility, foresight, action, and decisiveness.

It was the last three of these—foresight, action, and decisiveness—that caused a wave of anxiety to wash over me because I realized that I wasn't exhibiting any of these traits as a mom, especially in relation to what could be a very serious problem with my son. After berating myself for having been so lazy and complacent, I took Machiavelli's insights to heart and immediately sought expert medical advice, something that I should have done at a much earlier point in time.

And when I finally got off my rump, showed a little virtù, and talked with some doctors, I soon learned that all would be well. As good fortune would have it, Trevor's speech began to rapidly develop as soon as he entered preschool, which was obviously a huge relief to my husband and me. And by the time our first parent-teacher conference rolled around, he was talking almost as well as his peers.

Yes, delayed speech can be a sign of a serious problem that requires timely treatment to effectively combat—but not always. Legend has it that Albert Einstein didn't start talking until he was five, and when he was later asked why, he supposedly replied, "I didn't have anything to say."

Today, just like that cute little girl at the park, it seems like Trevor *never* stops talking—which is perfectly fine with me because since I once thought that he might not ever speak or that I might not ever hear him say "Mommy," his sweet little voice is like a symphony to me.

My son grew into his voice, and as he did, I grew, too, for I learned yet another lesson from Machiavelli, one that applied as much to me as it did to my kids. With this in mind, I resolved that should a potentially serious issue arise in the future with any of my kids (or with myself), I would act with foresight and decisiveness. And I would immediately dispatch whatever forces might be necessary to combat it.

Bottom line: Stop procrastinating. Get out of denial mode. And whatever you do, don't let problems develop until they're obvious to everyone. That's not only bad leadership. It can be devastating for a prince—and disastrous for a mom and her kids.

IX

*One Who Becomes a Prince
Through the Favor of the People
Ought to Keep Them Friendly:*
Sometimes, the Best Way to
Enforce a Rule Is to Break It

It was now seven months into my little Machiavellian plan. And I'd seen some nice changes in my brood. Teddy and Daniel were happy, well mannered, and doing well in school. Katie was happy, joyful, and behaving better, though she still had the frustrating habit of running away. And Trevor was talking up a storm at preschool. We'd come a long way. Still, there was much work to do. So having just made such major changes, I decided it was time to tackle one more. The issue: sleeping arrangements.

This, for my family, was a critical issue, as it influenced all others. Not only did it directly affect how all of us felt each day, it had a direct impact on our daily family dynamics. This, of course, came out most clearly in my relationship with my husband. Because not only were we rarely sharing a marital bed—if you get my drift—we both felt totally overwhelmed, exhausted, frustrated, defeated, and stressed-out. And I'm not kidding when I say that herding a litter of feral kittens would've been easier than getting our little minions into their respective bedrooms for a full night's sleep.

Am I the only mom who is so woefully ad hoc and lackadaisical (a harsher critic might say "incompetent") about setting a strict bedtime ritual that gets (and keeps) my kids to bed at a decent, consistent time each night? Based on anecdotal discussions with friends, I don't think so. But the issue of bedtime and sleeping arrangements is one that often isn't discussed outside families and close friends. And no matter what kind of bedtime rules you choose, there's a lot of judgment and guilt out there.

Co-sleep in a family bed? You're putting your child's safety at risk.

Put them in their own room? You obviously don't love your little ones.

Can't wrangle them into bed at a consistent time each night? You know you're setting them up for a lifetime of sleep deprivation and underachievement.

I know all parents struggle with bedtime, but the sleeping arrangements in my house seemed to be particularly chaotic. A typical night at our place might find Katie galloping around the house like friggin' Seabiscuit at eleven o'clock, while Trevor was snuggled up in the master bedroom with Eric, whose intermittent fits of sonic boom–like snores would invariably drive me downstairs.

There, I might find Teddy sleeping soundly on our couch, and I would doze off around midnight while reading in the chair right beside her . . . which, while comforting to her (she didn't like to sleep in her room, but more on that later), had caused a pesky crick in my neck and chronic sense of sleep deprivation.

"Someone please shoot me, now!" I mumbled to myself early one morning, after yet another night of repeatedly interrupted sleep. "The madness has to *stop!*"

But I didn't know *how* to stop it. So I decided to apply some of the Machiavellian principles that had worked so well in other areas of our lives. Remember that earlier rule: a good ruler sets limits? Sounds like a good plan in tackling this problem, too. So I gathered my family together again and firmly established the new rule of "Quiet Time." Every night at exactly 8:45, I'd turn down the lights. This did get my kids to calm down a bit. For a while. But soon 8:45 turned to 9:00, which somehow got pushed back to 10:00— and within a few weeks our nightly life was just as crazy and chaotic as before. Machiavelli seemed to be no match for my midnight brigade.

Desperate to win this battle, I did what many beleaguered moms and dads might do: I began issuing threats and ultimatums. "If you're not in bed in *exactly* three minutes," I'd proclaim, "we're *never* going to Baskin-Robbins again!"

But of course these ultimatums inevitably backfired and my empty threats only further diminished my credibility and power. Strong rules were failing me. Positive reinforcement wasn't cutting it. All of my previously foolproof

Machiavellian tricks just weren't working. In other words, like General George B. McClellan, who couldn't manage his own troops at Antietam, I was on the brink of a massive and seemingly irrevocable defeat. And as I pondered my own troops' fate, I remembered that McClellan's greatest strategic failing was that he had devoted himself to not losing rather than to winning. And that is never an effective strategy for any leader—be it a general, a prince, a boss, or a mom.

But what is an embattled leader to do?

Taking my cue from Machiavelli, I knew I had to take a commanding new stand, which I did by acting decisively, waging my battle on three fronts.

First, I told Trevor that he had to begin sleeping in his own bed, an order that he bristled against with a torrent of terrible, heart-wrenching tears. But I was determined to win this war, even if it meant sitting next to him for two hours each night until he finally dozed off in utter toddlerhood exhaustion. As it turns out, that's exactly what it meant.

Next, I broke the news to Teddy that she, too, had to sleep in her own room, a rule rendered even more oppressive since she was still sleeping in her dad's bedroom whenever she stayed with him.

Finally, it was time to set my sights on Seabiscuit, and I decided that, for her own safety, and everyone's sanity,

I would let her fall asleep with a TV playing quietly in her room. I know—for this alone I won't be nominated as Mom of the Year. But while this pragmatic Machiavellian plan did put an end to her late-night galloping antics, it also created a new problem. Because Katie happily responded by playing her favorite *Muppets Take Manhattan* DVD on repeat, cranking up the volume to a deafening decibel level of 83—at three a.m. Soon, regular late-night eruptions of "Am I a Man or Am I a Muppet?" would jolt the whole house awake, leaving all of us crabby, cranky, and totally exhausted the next day.

Clearly, this situation called for some advanced Machiavellian techniques. So, after dropping Teddy off at her elementary school, taking Katie to day care, and dashing across town to deliver Trevor twenty minutes late to preschool, I groggily collapsed on the couch with *The Prince*, seeking some insight—and what I read this time was frightening.

"And it ought to be remembered," Machiavelli cautions, "that there is nothing more difficult to take in hand, more perilous to conduct, or more uncertain in its success, than to take the lead in the introduction of a new order of things."

Gee, thanks for the reminder, I thought with dark bags under my eyes. Of course, I'd been doing nothing *but* instituting a new order of things for the last several months. But bedtime was different, stubbornly resisting the Machiavellian magic that had transformed some other aspects of our lives. Still, I knew I had to institute new bedtime rules that actually resulted in restful nights, and sooner rather than later—for my own sanity, as well as that of my tired family (and my ever-more-frustrated husband).

And that's when I remembered a passage in *The Prince* wherein Machiavelli examines the relationship between the people (or, in my house, the kids) and the nobles (Eric and me). He describes these two groups as constantly at odds, but his sympathy is clearly with the people, who, he says, "only ask to be free from oppression."

Reminding his readers that people in republics like Florence had valued their freedom above all else, and that they were totally justified in doing so, he goes on to say that a leader must win over the people because they are many, while the nobles are few, and that a prince can never live safely without the trust of his subjects.

That sounds more like a democracy than a tyranny, right?

But this is where things start to get hairy because Machiavelli warns that "in all cities it arises that the people do not wish to be ruled nor oppressed by the nobles, and the nobles wish to rule and oppress the people; and from these two opposite desires there arises in cities one of three results, either a principality, self-government, or anarchy."

Anarchy? Please! That's the last thing I need!

Fearing a rebellion if not full-blown revolt, I knew I had to retreat and revise my strategy, which I quickly did by shifting my emphasis from my own desire to enforce orders to my kids' desire to be free from oppression. Here I was taking my cue again from Machiavelli, who says that "one who becomes a prince through the favor of the people ought to keep them friendly, and this he can easily do see-ing they only ask not to be oppressed by him."

That's important, I thought, for both a prince and a mom. It was also directly helpful because it was a clear, practical maxim that I could work with and implement in a way that would get me—and my kids—some much-needed sleep.

Machiavelli's maxim, as I chose to interpret it, was this: "One who becomes a prince through the favor of the people ought to keep them friendly."

Sounds simple enough, right? I mean, my kids only asked to be free to sleep where they felt safe and secure, which was justifiable. But the key word is: *sleep.* Not gig-gling. Not galloping. Not blasting Kermit the Frog at three in the morning. There had to be a way to give them some freedom in the matter and still remain sane.

So, after much thought, I softened my stance. And as I began to relax, I remembered that Machiavelli is all about flexibility. In fact, he believed that flexibility is the most crucial virtù a leader can have, especially in times of crisis. On this, he says that a leader must always be willing and able to change course if that's what's demanded in any given situation. Yes, he gives us the basic tools, or master plan, for rules, discipline, and domination . . . but he also tells us that sometimes it's wiser to retreat than to fight a losing battle. Armed with these insights, I finally devised a win-ning strategy, which was this: I would be firm but flexible while keeping my kids' happiness (and everyone's sanity) at bedtime at the forefront of my mind.

In the end, I didn't so much wave the white flag or capitulate to any unreasonable demands as simply appease my children's basic nocturnal wants and needs. Which, in short order, meant that Teddy began sleeping on our comfy old couch again, and I dozed off while reading in the chair right beside her. Meanwhile, Trevor and Katie, to their great relief, got to sleep cuddled up next to Eric. None of this would bode well for our once fantastic and very active sex life but, in the hierarchy of human needs, sleep narrowly beats out sex when it comes to individual human survival, right?

And besides, I made it perfectly clear that this wasn't a permanent arrangement. Instead, I promised my kids that they could continue sleeping this way only if they promised in exchange to begin sleeping in their own rooms no later than Halloween (okay, Thanksgiving), which was about two months away. And, as a lawyer, I knew that this was a valid and binding, legally enforceable oral agreement. Offer. Acceptance. Consideration. Got 'em!

With this longer lead time established, and a clear transition in sight, you know what? It worked. And by Thanksgiving, everyone was (mostly) in their own beds, and we were all (mostly) getting a peaceful night's sleep.

Bottom line: I ultimately got what I wanted out of my kids, and they thought it was their idea because they helped create the agreement! In other words, it's all about power. You've got it. But if they think they do, you're golden.

PART II

The Experiment Goes Awry

While enlightening, my little sleeping experiment—and my experiment with Machiavelli as a whole—had left me feeling somewhat exhausted. So I decided to take a quick break from *The Prince* to find out what Machiavelli's intent was in writing it. And what I stumbled across was a question that has baffled some of the world's greatest philosophers and scholars for nearly five hundred years. That question: Did the author of *The Prince* write it as a satire, or did he really mean what he wrote?

Wait, *what*? Had I been basing my whole family's well-being on a joke?

Among the Enlightenment philosophers of Europe,

French philosopher Jean-Jacques Rousseau believed that Machiavelli's masterpiece was, indeed, satire. How do I know this? Because in his *Social Contract* he wrote:

> *Machiavelli was a proper man and a good citizen; but, being attached to the court of the Medici, he could not help veiling his love of liberty in the midst of his country's oppression. The choice of his detestable hero, Caesar Borgia, clearly enough shows his hidden aim . . . this profound political thinker has so far been studied only by superficial or corrupt readers. The Court of Rome sternly prohibited his book. I can well believe it; for it is that Court it most clearly portrays.*

Okay, so what Rousseau seems to be saying here is that perhaps Machiavelli—with both the Medicis and the Church eyeing him with equal suspicion—couldn't write openly about the corruption he saw and had to write a satire to cover his ass. That's plausible, right? Because if the Medicis thought he was mocking them, they could have and probably would have quickly tossed him back in prison and tortured him again—or hired a hit man.

So that's one theory.

But more recent observers, I learned, believe that Machiavelli wasn't a satirist at all but a deadly serious political strategist who offered carefully crafted advice designed to bring about the ruin of Lorenzo de' Medici if taken seriously and followed. But this little plan—if it was, in fact, his plan—didn't pan out. Why? Because the Medicis probably didn't even read *The Prince*, and even if they did, they weren't morons and wouldn't have trusted its author, whose staunch republican sympathies were well known. And besides, the Medicis were well aware of the fact that their return to power in 1512 had triggered the beginning of all of Machiavelli's problems.

But this last fact, I thought, would support a satirical intent, as historian Garrett Mattingly argues in his widely cited article "Machiavelli's *Prince*: Political Science or Political Satire?" "I suppose it is possible," Mattingly caustically posits, "to imagine that a man who has seen his country enslaved, his life's work wrecked and his own career with it, and has, for good measure, been tortured within an inch of his life, should thereupon go home and write a book intended to teach his enemies the proper way to maintain themselves, writing all the time, with the passionless objectivity of a scientist in a laboratory. It must be possible to imagine such behavior," he adds, "because Machiavelli scholars do imagine it and accept it without a visible tremor. But it is a little difficult for the ordinary mind to compass."

Ouch. But he's right—the "state" that Machiavelli's treatise was supposed to help was in fact the very one that had made his life a living hell for so many years. In fact, in all the rest of his writing throughout his career, Machiavelli made it abundantly clear that he hated tyrannies. So . . . why would he write a guidebook for tyrants unless he didn't really mean what he wrote?

Uh-oh, I thought, suddenly doubting myself. Is *The Prince* just one big satirical joke? And if it is, is the joke now squarely on me?

Desperate for answers, I began scrambling to find out

what, if anything, Machiavelli had to say for himself. And that's when I discovered a startling letter he wrote near the end of his life. "For some time now I have never said what I believe, nor ever believed what I said," he confessed, "and if indeed I do sometimes tell the truth, I hide it behind so many lies that it is hard to find."

Houston, we have a problem!

Did we ever.

X

Consider Whether an Action's Perils Exceed Its Advantages:
Picking Your Battles

Greet Madonna Marietta for me and tell her I have been expecting—
and still do—to leave here any day; I have never longed so much
to return to Florence as I do now, but there is nothing else I can
do. Simply tell her that, whatever she hears, she should be of good
cheer, since I shall be there before any danger comes.

> Machiavelli, letter to his son Guido, 1527

Energized—and well rested!—I decided to temporarily shift my attention from my kids to my husband, who I love dearly but who, for most of his adult life, has always been the proverbial last guy to leave the bar. And after we tied the knot, he didn't exactly change his late-night ways, at least when he was away on business trips. He'd stay out partying with his colleagues until well past midnight, sometimes until one or two a.m.

"I'm trying to close a deal," he chirped into his cell phone in some loud, crowded bar.

"Right," I sighed. "But why don't you just close your tab, honey, and call it a night?"

Like my husband, Machiavelli traveled frequently on business. As a respected but relatively obscure diplomat in the Florentine republic (think US ambassador to Tahiti), he took trips in various capacities to one or another location in Tuscany, and, on numerous occasions between 1498 and 1512, he acted as an envoy on extended missions in France, Germany, Spain, and elsewhere in Europe. He also met regularly with Pope Alexander VI and the newly crowned King Louis XII and visited the camps of Cesare Borgia, the cruel, cunning, and vicious Duke of Valentinois, whose character and career greatly influenced Machiavelli's political thought and provided the basis for his opinions on leadership that he would later set forth so clearly and crisply in *The Prince*.

Machiavelli was also married during these years. In 1502, at the age of thirty-two, he married Marietta Corsini, who bore him six healthy children. And while their marriage was most likely an arranged one, as most Florentine marriages were at the time, it is clear from her letters that Marietta had great love for her husband and his prolonged absences no doubt weighed heavily on her, especially when their children were young. "Remember to come home," she wrote in a letter to him shortly after the birth of their first son.

"Remember to come home" are haunting words for a wife to write to her husband—and revealing ones. But with all of Italy torn by war among rival factions and with

Machiavelli surrounded by personal and political enemies, Marietta had good reason to worry for her husband's safety when he was away. And one can only wonder if she also didn't worry that he might one day take a transient mistress or two, something that I learned from his letters he did, in fact, do.

What happens in Rome stays in Rome. Right?

In this, I could empathize with Marietta because, like I said, my husband frequently traveled when our kids were young. Unlike Machiavelli, however, Eric is in the golf industry and whenever he went on a trip, he and his equally hardworking, fun-loving colleagues liked to relax and live large. Their days often began with Bloody Marys before teeing off, followed by who knows how many beers delivered to them by perky young "beer-cart girls" on the course. They'd then polish off the afternoon with cocktails at the "19th Hole" (read: clubhouse bar), followed by a few vodkas on the rocks and glasses of wine at dinner, after which the party duly moved to yet another bar.

One year, Eric went on his annual business trip to a golf tournament in Puerto Vallarta, and every night, for five consecutive nights, he stayed out partying with his colleagues until the wee hours of the morning. Don't get me wrong: I'm not some puritanical, teetotaling Pollyanna. I can drink with the best of them (and frequently did in my pre-parenthood days). And I could understand if he stayed out late on a few of the nights. But five consecutive days downing beer after beer on a golf course followed by an endless flow of vodka and tequila shots? I mean, come on!

Not only is that not good for your marriage, it's not good for your liver.

The first year he went on this particular trip, Trevor was four months old and still breast-feeding, and so while Eric was out mingling with dozens of sexy young "Cuervo girls" with their bodacious double-D tatas spilling out of their teeny-weeny bikini tops, I was home alone breast-feeding an infant and caring for two toddlers in my tattered old, expandable-waist, post-pregnancy sweatpants.

A Cuervo girl I was not.

But that was five years ago. And I didn't particularly mind, because I always want him to have a good time. But, like Marietta, I often worried about my husband's safety when he was away—and I also worried that he might one night, in an inebriated state, do something that might betray me and our marriage.

What happens in Rome stays in Rome. Yeah, sorry, Machiavelli, that's not going to fly with me.

With this troubling scenario in mind, I finally decided that I would no longer support Eric's late-night drinking sprees. It didn't matter where in the world he was. Puerto Vallarta. Florida. New York. Canada, Cancún, or Colorado. I was done playing the role of the long-suffering wife who was always home alone caring for kids and waiting anxiously for a late-night phone call that invariably never came.

Fortunately, Eric manned up and promised to change his behavior. He also agreed to call or text me to let me know that he had returned safely to his hotel room at the end of the night.

Then he went to Las Vegas for a PGA golf merchandise show.

It was a Thursday night and I had fallen asleep while reading downstairs in a chair. When I woke, it was two a.m. I assumed I had missed his call. But when I checked my cell phone there was no voice mail, so I called him.

"Where are you?" I asked flatly when he answered.

"At the craps table," he said cheerfully, clearly oblivious to my growing anger.

"With who? Doug and John?"

"Uh, no," he mumbled. "Two fashion writers I met today at the show."

Fashion writers? I thought as my blood began to boil. How many men in the golf industry write about Tiger's new visors and cleats?

"Let me guess," I said. "They're women?"

"Uh, yeah," he said sheepishly. "They want to write for my magazine."

And that's when I lost it.

"What the *hell* are you doing out drinking at two a.m. with two women you just met? What would you do if you called me at two in the morning and I was out partying with two men I just met at a lawyers' convention in Vegas?"

Mount Vesuvius was about to erupt. And he knew it.

"I'm sorry, honey," he quickly offered. "I get it. You have a right to be upset."

When he came home the next day, I told him again that I understood he had to travel for business and that I would continue to support that, but I would no longer support what I deemed to be immature, frat-boy behavior. He agreed that his behavior was destructive to our marriage and again promised to change his ways.

But old habits die hard, especially ones that are fun.

This time he was in San Diego. He called at six p.m. to say that he was meeting the CEO of a tee-time company (who is also a friend) for a quick dinner and would go back to his hotel right after that. He didn't. And when he hadn't called by midnight, I called him. No answer. I waited another hour and called again. And, again, no answer.

Maybe he's asleep and doesn't hear his phone ringing, I thought, giving him the benefit of the doubt. But by two a.m. and a dozen more unanswered calls, I was once again wide-awake in the wee hours of the night wondering where the hell my husband was.

Eric finally called at nine the next morning. He had too much wine at dinner, he said, and instead of driving, he stayed on the couch in his friend's hotel room.

"I can't do this anymore," I said decisively and hung up.

And that wasn't an empty threat or ultimatum. It was an essential and definitive decision. In this, I was taking my cue from Machiavelli. "It is well in all deliberations to come at once to the essential point," he advises, "and not always to remain in a state of indecision and uncertainty." However long I had remained in a state of indecision and uncertainty, I had at last come to the "essential point" in my own marital deliberations.

When Eric returned home later that day, he apologized

profusely, told me that he had been selfish, and once again assured me that he'd never do it again. I listened calmly to him and then told him again that I was done. With his behavior, and with our marriage.

But no sooner had I delivered this dire proclamation than considerations of no small magnitude quickly arose in my mind.

Our children were young and I didn't want to put them through the pain of a separation or divorce. Plus, I was deeply in love with my husband, however seemingly great and wide-ranging his flaws.

Torn with indecision, I referred again to my trusty old copy of *The Prince.* This time I read Machiavelli's admonishment: "Before deciding upon any course, men should consider the objections and dangers it presents, and if its perils exceed the advantages, they should avoid it, even though it had been in accordance with their previous determination."

And as I thought about this, I remembered my own advice as a divorce lawyer that I often dispensed to potential clients, which was this: short of physical or emotional abuse, infidelity, or serious drug or alcohol abuse, don't file for divorce unless you're prepared to live with the consequences. If you're not prepared to see your soon-to-be-former husband or wife dating or remarried, and if you're not ready to live the rest of your life without them, don't file for divorce. It's okay and maybe even healthy and cathartic to think about it long and hard. But don't do it. Divorce is a major decision, one of the biggest you can make in your life, and it has far-reaching and permanent ramifications, not only for yourself but for your children.

Like Marietta's marriage to Machiavelli, my marriage to Eric isn't perfect and never will be. But having once come to the essential point of deciding to leave my marriage, I considered the objections and dangers it presented, and because its perils (a broken heart, sharing custody of our children) exceeded its advantages (no more lost sleep over late-night phone calls), I avoided it, even though it had been in accordance with my previous determination.

After some time had passed, I told Eric that he didn't have to let me know when he returned to his hotel room at the end of the night. "If you call or text, great," I said. "If you don't, it doesn't matter."

"It does matter," he said firmly. "And I will call because it's the right thing to do."

And you know what? He does.

Despite his fun-loving and sometimes infuriating late-night ways, my husband is a very loyal and loving husband, and I am totally committed to him and our children. And should I ever get so fed up again as to seriously contemplate divorce, I will, as Machiavelli advises, consider the dangers it presents, and if its perils outweigh its advantages, I shall avoid it.

Once again, Machiavelli had helped me strategically wage—or, more accurately, successfully avoid—a major battle, and, if he were here with me today, I would thank him for that. And then I'd give him a quick kick in the ass on Marietta's behalf for his marital infidelities and indiscretions.

"What happens in Rome doesn't always stay in Rome," I would advise him. "And that is a maxim you can live by."

XI

The Best Fortress a Prince Can Possess Is the Affection of the People:
Strengthening the Ties That Bind

With the rough edges of my marriage ironed out (for now), I turned my attention back to my kids. Things were pretty good at home—better, certainly, than they had been at the start of this little experiment. The kids were, more often than not, behaving. Homework got done mostly on time. Tantrums were down dramatically. Sleep was happening, and usually in everyone's own bed. So, what next?

A prince shouldn't kick back and rest on his laurels, Machiavelli says. Even in peaceful times—in fact, especially in peaceful times—it is incumbent upon a good ruler to always be alert for ways to keep his subjects happy and content. On this, he says that a leader must be ever vigilant to win and keep the affection of the people, not for the sake of their affection itself, but to "ensure the security of a state in the face of a potential siege by foreign invaders."

A siege in Machiavelli's day was a much more dangerous undertaking than breaking up food fights and siblings' spats, I know. We're talking about lengthy affairs, during which invading armies would camp outside the fortified walls of a city for weeks or even months in an attempt to starve out or crush the will of the people. In these cases, a prince is left with only two options: wait out the siege or hope for assistance from an ally. But in either case, a prince isn't in such a pinch so long as he has adequate provisions and keeps up the spirit of his people. Or, as Machiavelli puts it, "The best fortress a prince can possess is the affection of the people," because without that "a prince has no security in adversity."

While I've never been overly concerned about a potential siege by my neighbors (although, now that I think of it, Wayne did shoot me a disgruntled look one day last May when I was finally getting around to taking down my Christmas lights), I did agree that it's wise for a leader to maintain the affection of his people. And Machiavelli makes a valid point: if you've worked hard to win the affection of your subjects in good times, they're more likely to stick with you in bad times. (And believe me, bad times were coming, though I didn't know it yet.)

This is another central principle in *The Prince* and, after carefully writing it on our List, I set out to build up a little "fortress of affection" with my own loyal subjects.

With this benevolent but no less strategic piece of advice in mind, I decided to bestow upon my kids a very special gift they had been petitioning to receive for years. And after a lengthy search, I presented them with a rambunctious little black runt of a kitten, with impossibly long fluffy black fur, bright copper eyes, and a crooked front tooth that jutted out of her mouth like the fang of a saber-toothed tiger.

Ecstatic, my kids played with her endlessly, and soon Blackie became a beloved new member of our family—which was all well and good until she suddenly developed a nasty habit of occasionally relieving herself smack-dab in the center of Eric's pillow.

Normally I would assume, as most loving pet owners would naturally do, that this was an isolated event, that she had somehow gotten locked in the room with no suitable place for refuse. But, after consulting with our vet and diligently putting into effect all of his recommendations, Blackie continued to make a statement on Eric's pillow—and it quickly became clear that this wasn't just a simple case of aberrant feline behavior but a deliberate siege, a ruthless and rebellious plan of attack.

Reluctant but disgusted, I realized that I had only two options: give her away or let her stay outside during the day. Mindful of the need to maintain my subjects' affection, I chose the latter, which not only solved the immediate crisis but solidified the affection of Blackie, too, who was reveling in the many surprises and delights of her newfound liberty and freedom. *Birds! Sun! Butterflies! Lizards! And an endless supply of fresh dirt!*

This idyllic state of affairs continued until I discovered one late winter day that our sweet innocent little kitten had grown into a cat and had gotten herself irresponsibly knocked up. Okay, so maybe I was the irresponsible party here. But I honestly thought that her previous owner had had her neutered before I'd adopted her and brought her home.

Clearly, this wasn't the case.

But there's no use in arguing over spilled milk, right? Besides, my kids were thrilled by the idea of having lots of cute cuddly little kittens chasing each other playfully around the house. So we waited with great anticipation for the big day to arrive.

"Guess what?" I said as I was making scrambled eggs in the kitchen while Teddy was reading on my Kindle.

"What?" she said without looking up.

"Blackie had her kittens."

"She did?"

"Yep."

"YAY!" she shrieked. "Can we see them?"

I nodded, then led my subjects up to the master bedroom, where they kneeled down on the floor and peered into a large box in the corner of the closet.

"How many did she have?" Teddy whispered.

"Three."

"Three little kittens!" she laughed. "Just like the book!" Then she looked up at me and asked, "Can we name them?"

"Sure," I said, pointing at the tiny gray one. "What should we name that one?"

"Smokey," she said decisively.

"Perfect."

I pointed at a white one that was much bigger. "And how about that guy?"

"Uh . . . Mucho Macho Man!"

"How'd you get that?" I asked.

"It's the name of a horse you let me bet on last year when you and Eric took us to the track."

Great, another item to add to my list of parental vices and sins.

"Okay," I nodded.

"Can I pick up that one?" she asked, pointing at a tiny orange one that was clearly the runt.

"Just be gentle," I cautioned.

"And this is Orange Guy," she whispered. Then she cuddled him close to her chest and asked, "What's your favorite one?"

"Orange Guy," I replied.

"Why?"

"Because he's the runt."

She giggled and gently stroked his soft fur. "Me, too."

Affection won! I thought, and as an image of Machiavelli's enigmatic half smile crossed my mind, Teddy turned to me and sadly asked, "Can we give one to Dad?"

"Dad? Sure. Why?"

"So he won't be lonely when I'm not with him."

I nodded but didn't respond.

"I mean, you have Eric, Trevor, Katie, Daniel, and Blackie

when I'm not here," she said in a voice barely above a whisper. "But Dad only has Ben."

"A man's best friend is his dog," I said, trying to keep her spirits up. "Besides, I think your dad likes being alone."

"I know," she said slowly, "but I don't want him to be alone."

And that's the thing about Teddy: she's the most thoughtful, caring, and sensitive individual of any age I have ever known. I don't know where she got that from. But I do know that she loves her dad and me more than anything and that her greatest hope was that we would one day get back together again.

I also know that one of my greatest fears as her mother was that even though Paul and I now share equal custody of her, she would one day want to live with him instead of me. And perhaps that's why Machiavelli's admonishment that a prince must maintain the affection of his people had such a deep and melancholy resonance for me. My desire to maintain my daughter's affection was driven by my fear of losing it—and her—someday.

In this sense, Machiavelli's rule wasn't so much about bestowing special gifts on my kids as it was about the sometimes painful tug-of-war that parents (both together and separated) play for the affections of their children. For me, this means many overnight and long weekend good-byes. It also means knowing that I won't be physically present in Teddy's life for nearly nine of the first eighteen years of her life—and that she won't be physically present in mine for that same staggering amount of time. And so I suppose it's that hard fact that not only heightens but makes very real my primal fear of losing my daughter and her affection.

And if you're a divorced mother of a young child, or even if you're not, you know what I'm talking about. Being a mom is being in a state of constant fear. Because we're just one phone call, one solemn knock on the door, one malignant twist of fate away from total devastation and heartbreak. And that, my friend, is a fate we can't ever escape. So what do we do? Machiavelli would tell us to accept it as a given, buck up, and forge on!

Like many marriages that collapse and end in ruin, the collapse and ruin of my marriage to Teddy's father was triggered and fueled by many long, slowly smoldering and short, fast-burning fuses. But there's always more than one side to every story, so I won't bother you with that. What matters here is that even though Paul and I had been divorced for many years when I hatched my Machiavellian plan, Teddy was still struggling to come to terms with it. The depth of her sadness found voice in a poem she recently wrote, entitled "I AM." Now hanging prominently on the wall of her third-grade classroom, it reads:

> *I am Teddy King.*
> *I wonder why my parents got divorced.*
> *I hear my kitten meowing.*

I see myself skiing.
I want another dog.
I am an animal lover.

I pretend I'm skiing off the top of
     Mammoth Mountain.
I feel my dog's fur.
I touch my kitty's fluffy fur.
I cry to my dog why my parents got
     divorced.
I am going to be an awesome skier.

I understand the rules of soccer.
I say to myself why my parents got
     divorced.
I try to be the fastest swimmer.
I try to do my best in math.
I hope that my parents will get back
     together.
I am Teddy King.

I swallowed hard as I read it for the first time at Open House. And I as read some of the other students' poems, I couldn't help but notice that while most of her classmates were defining themselves in terms of their own unique wants and needs, many of which evoked such simple childhood pleasures as ice cream cones, baseball games, and family picnics, Teddy was primarily defining herself by her lingering confusion and grief over her parents' divorce.

"Do you like being married more to Dad or Eric?" she asked one morning, as she has many times, as I was driving her to school.

"It's different," I said, as I always do.

"I know," she persisted, "but *how* is it different?"

"Well," I said, trying to think of something I hadn't already told her. "In some ways it was easier being married to your dad, because he helped a lot around the house and paid all the bills."

"So you liked being married more to Dad than Eric!" she proclaimed, as if to say, like Perry Mason, "I rest my case."

"But," I continued, "Eric and I have something together that your dad and I never had."

"Like what?"

"Like, he makes me laugh a lot and we're more compatible."

"But you argue a lot."

"Yeah, we do," I acknowledged.

"Did you have a lot of arguments with Dad?"

"No," I said softly.

"How many times did you argue?" she asked, clearly intrigued with this compelling new information, which would surely help solidify her case.

"Maybe once or twice," I replied as I slowed to a stop in the long line of cars waiting to turn into the parking lot.

"Then that's good," she smiled.

"Not necessarily," I said, "because if you don't ever argue, your problems grow bigger and bigger until one day they're so big, they can't ever be resolved."

As I pulled up to the curb, she got silent and stared out the window as if her mind were a million miles away.

"What are you thinking about?" I finally asked.

She grabbed her backpack, then looked at me and said very matter-of-factly, "Rainbows and unicorns."

D'oh! I thought, and as I watched her slide out of the car and disappear in the crowd of teachers and students, my stomach clenched up in knots. And as I drove slowly home, I worried that I had made her even more confused than she'd been before.

XII

Don't Abandon What Is for What Should Be:
Accepting the Reality in Front of You

We are much beholden to Machiavelli and others, that write what men do, and not what they ought to do.

Francis Bacon

I thought again about Machiavelli's maxim that a prince must possess the affection of the people. I guess I'd originally thought that preserving the affection of my kids was a way to build up a strong "fortress" around us and keep our family (and my power in the family) safe. Which was all well and good—the kittens had been a big hit. But I was realizing that no matter how many kittens or special gifts I might bring home, there were some deeper fissures in my fortress and in my family as a whole.

Did the dissolution of my first marriage mean that I'd always have a deep structural weakness in the "fortress" of my new family? Would there be endless power struggles—

and endless struggles for Teddy's affection—between her father and me? Worse, would she always feel torn in her own affection and even love for us? And would she forever be grieving the "ideal family" that she was dreaming of having but had lost?

Tough issues for any parent to confront. But, as it turns out, the ever-pragmatic Machiavelli has some words of advice that help out here, too. In particular, he claims explicitly throughout *The Prince* that he's not interested in talking about ideal republics or imaginary utopias, as many of his predecessors had done. On this point, he writes, "Many men have imagined republics and principalities that never really existed at all, yet the way men live is so far removed from the way they ought to live that anyone who abandons what is for what should be pursues his downfall rather than his preservation." In other words, don't pine for what should or could have been. Deal with the reality in front of you.

This belief, this tough-minded realism, is at the heart of Machiavelli's political philosophy and is, in part, what has caused so much vitriol and venom to spill from the lips of his critics. Much of his advice is notoriously shocking, to be sure, but what makes it even more shocking is the casual, matter-of-fact way in which he presents it.

Yet, as I thought about this, it hit me that the larger purpose of his realism isn't shocking or diabolical at all. And by that I mean he simply intends to warn a prince that it's dangerous to live as a fuzzy-minded idealist with his head stuck in the clouds (or somewhere else). Instead, he urges men to live in the real world, where rulers like Lorenzo de' Medici became great by practicing the cunning and ruthless use of power. To do anything less, to abandon what is for what should be, as Machiavelli pithily puts it, will lead to man's downfall rather than his preservation.

Viewing self-preservation as the better option, I decided it was time to face the facts and have a little heart-to-heart chat with Teddy.

"Can we talk for a second?" I asked as she was reading *Charlotte's Web* in her room.

"About what?" she asked.

"Me and Dad."

She smiled but looked sad. "Yeah," she said, closing the book.

I sat on the edge of her bed, then said, "So, I know how hard it is for you that Dad and I are divorced."

"Why'd you have to get divorced?" she asked. "None of my friends' parents are divorced."

"I know," I said softly, "and I can't tell you exactly why we got divorced. All I know is that by the time you were born, lots of problems had built up between us and—"

"Because you never argued?" she interrupted, trying to make sense of it.

"That didn't help." I nodded. "And, after almost ten years of being married, we weren't very good at living together anymore and realized we'd both be happier living apart."

"But you aren't always happy."

I nodded again, then replied, "No one's always happy, and, in fact, I think the happiest people in the world are the ones who can accept their life for how it is and not for how they think it should be."

"It's just hard for me," she whispered.

"I know," I sighed. "It was hard for me, too. But the best thing we can do is try to accept both the good and the bad in our lives and be grateful for what we have. Make sense?"

"Yeah," she shrugged, then pulled her beloved white furless stuffed kitten, Special Kitty, from under the covers. (This particular stuffed kitten was very special indeed because, as I had told Teddy many times, I bought it for comfort and good luck while undergoing infertility treatments years earlier and then slept with it every night until Teddy was born.)

"Special Kitty!" I smiled. "You hide her under your covers?"

"Yeah, so Katie can't find her."

"Good thinkin'," I said, then tucked her and Special Kitty into bed and kissed them both on the top of the head.

"Mom?" she whispered.

"Hmm?"

"Am I staying with you tomorrow night or with Dad?"

"Tomorrow's Wednesday, so Dad."

"All right," she smiled, then she held Special Kitty tight and got quiet for a while. "Remember, I really want to give a kitten to Dad so he's not lonely when I'm not with him," she finally said.

"Okay. Which one?"

"Whatever one he wants!" she said excitedly.

"All right," I smiled. "I think that's a fabulous idea."

Not long after our chat, Teddy's dad (a true dog lover at heart) agreed to adopt Mucho Macho Man. And while adopting a family cat might seem like a commonplace act, it ran much deeper than that for both Paul and me. Because it was a way of building a bridge between our two separate homes and it showed Teddy that we are both happier apart in our new lives than in our old one together. And even though I knew from Machiavelli that affection may wax and wane, I also knew that I could and would always work with her father to make sure that she always feels safe and secure and to help her accept her life for how it is as opposed to how she might think it should be.

In *The Prince* and his other works, Machiavelli not only explores political leadership but also probes the depths of human nature, observing that when stripped of power struggles, unfulfilled ambitions, and endless conflict, "there are only individual egos, crazy for love." And while a casual reader might be hard-pressed to find a love story in his little masterpiece, it is nevertheless there in his deep and abiding devotion to his beloved Florence.

In a similar way, this little book is my own love story for my kids. And by applying Machiavelli's insights in this particular instance, I had helped guide my daughter toward a more mature and realistic understanding and acceptance of our life together, however imperfect it might sometimes (okay, frequently) be.

Equally important, I had, with a little help from Machiavelli, shown her that my own fortress of love and affection for her will never wane, regardless of how many nights she might spend away from me and with her father. And that, I thought, is yet another great takeaway for all modern-day moms and dads, no matter if they're separated or together.

XIII

Is It Better to Be Feared Than Loved?
Testing the Limits of Machiavelli's Advice

Despite a few misfires, Machiavelli's advice was for the most part still working for us. I was back on a smooth path with my husband. Teddy was coming to terms with her new reality. And even Daniel was coming around. But because of Katie's special needs, the strategies of strict limits and discipline that were working with my other kids weren't as effective with her.

Still, progress had been made, so I decided it was time to reward my kids for their efforts. I wanted to surprise them with a treat or a reward that would show how much I appreciated all their efforts and hard work over these past many months. But as all parents know, it's a hard line to walk sometimes between gaining your kids' affection and spoiling them too much. So, with this in mind, I turned again to Machiavelli. This time I considered his warning on the dangers of liberality and indulgence, ones that have a direct impact on whether a prince is feared or loved.

"Nothing feeds upon itself as liberality does," Machiavelli cautions. "The more it is indulged, the fewer are the means to indulge it further. As a consequence, a prince becomes poor and contemptible or, to escape poverty, becomes rapacious and hateful."

Poor and contemptible? Rapacious and hateful? Whether this referred to me or my kids, all I could say was "No thanks!"

Hoping to avoid that fate at all costs, I referred again to *The Prince* and learned that the more liberal a prince is with his expenditures, the more impoverished he will inevitably become, and, to fund his extravagance, he will have to tax his subjects or seize their possessions, which will make him both hated and feared by his subjects.

That makes sense, right? But what is a prudent ruler to do?

Machiavelli tells us that if a leader is willing to be miserly he will come to be appreciated and even loved by his subjects as he need not burden them to maintain the state. But Machiavelli goes out of his way to say that a prince must occasionally reward the people with festive parties, carnivals, and other displays of civic pride, glory, and wealth. He's not saying this to try to buy the love of the people. And he's certainly not saying that being loved is the best way to maintain a state. He's simply saying that partying with the people from time to time keeps things nice and tidy.

With this in mind, I devised a simple and pragmatic Machiavellian plan that would allow me to reward my kids while still being miserly.

"Guess what?" I said one Friday afternoon after school.

"You and Dad are getting back together!" Teddy chirped.

"No," I laughed. "But since you've been helping out so much, I'm taking you somewhere fun today."

"We're going to Disneyland!!!" Teddy shrieked to her siblings.

"Not quite, but close."

"Where?"

"The Fun Zone."

"YAY!" Teddy screamed as Trevor and Katie squealed with excitement, and for good reason because, with the exception of Disneyland, the Fun Zone—with its color-ful Ferris wheel, countless candy stores, and deafening arcades—is every child's favorite place to have fun in Or-ange County . . . and every parent's worst nightmare. Okay, maybe just my worst nightmare. But I was willing to brave it once in a while for the sake of my kids, who absolutely adored the clamor and noise.

"Can we go to the arcade first?!" Teddy asked. "And can Daniel come?!"

"Sure," I said. "But Daniel's with his mom this week-end, so it's just us today."

When we arrived at the Fun Zone a half hour later,

I laid down the law at the front entrance of the arcade that's directly adjacent to the main turning basin of the Newport Bay.

"All right," I said firmly. "You each get three dollars in tokens."

"Mom! Three dollars?" Teddy protested. "How about ten?"

"How about two?" I said sternly.

"Okay, three," she sighed.

"And everyone stays by my side the *whole* time," I said even more sternly.

"All right," Teddy said as Trevor nodded and stuck his thumb in his mouth.

"And, Katie," I said, staring her square in the eye. "You have to stay *right* by my side the whole time. Do you understand?" Her wandering spirit had been increasing recently, at home and (more troubling) at kindergarten. She'd already been asked to leave one school for her Count of Monte Cristo–like jailbreaking skills, and I feared we were on thin ice with her new school, too. "Don't go anywhere without me, okay?" I firmly repeated my command.

She giggled excitedly as I grabbed her hand.

"Okay," I said, taking a deep breath. "Let's go!"

Bright lights were flashing and loud bells were ringing as I helped Trevor and Katie toss skee balls up a ramp, and not more than five minutes had passed when Teddy tugged on the sleeve of my shirt and held up her empty cup.

"Can I have some more tokens, Mom, *please*?" she begged.

"All right," I sighed. "You can have mine." I turned

around, grabbed my cup, and emptied a few tokens into her cup. And when I turned back around a few seconds later, I saw Trevor standing dutifully by my side . . . but Katie was nowhere in sight.

Only her empty cup was left behind.

"Katie!" I shouted as I scanned the arcade. "Oh my god! Do you see her?"

Teddy shook her head, suddenly fearful and anxious.

I frantically scanned the arcade again, then picked up Trevor, grabbed Teddy's hand, and plowed through the crowd toward the docks.

"Katie!" I shouted.

"Katie!" Teddy called out after me.

Getting jostled and bumped, Trevor began crying, and Teddy couldn't keep up.

"Mom! Slow down," she pleaded.

"Hurry!" I screamed. "Please!"

"I can't," she said. "My stomach hurts."

Out of breath, I passed by a young mother pushing a stroller. "Have you seen a little girl? Red pants? Blond hair? Angry Birds shirt?"

"Sorry," she said, shaking her head.

Oh my god, I thought as I plowed through the crowd of tourists. And just as we reached the Ferris wheel, three loud warning sounds of a yacht rang out and I spun around and looked out, terrified, at the bay.

"What if she fell in the water?" Teddy whispered, knowing that Katie couldn't swim.

And that's when I lost it. "I have to call 911," I mumbled as I fumbled around in my purse for my cell phone.

And just when I found my phone, Teddy pointed toward the arcade and said, "There she is."

Sure enough, there was Katie, standing in front of a candy shop right next to the arcade.

"Katie!" I shouted as my heart pounded with equal parts terror and relief.

And as she giggled and pointed at a huge pink cone of cotton candy, I realized that my miserliness was what had created the crisis. But in that moment I wasn't thinking about culpability or cause. I was just a terrified and slightly traumatized mom who was very angry with her defiant young daughter. And once we got back to the car, I totally lost it.

"I told you to stay *right* by my side the whole time!" I shouted as I buckled Katie's car seat. "Teddy and Trevor always listen and obey! But *you* never listen to *anything* I say! And I can't take it anymore!"

Katie looked up at me, terrified.

As my blood pressure soared, I slammed my door, then glanced back at Teddy and Trevor and saw that they were really terrified, too . . . and as we drove home in total silence, my heart broke a little. Did I really want my children to fear me? Is this what it means to be a Machiavellian mom? And if so, is it worth it?

This wasn't just a onetime thing. Regardless of whatever rules or advice I applied, I couldn't keep Katie from misbehaving. It was getting to the point that whenever I would take her somewhere—the Fun Zone, the grocery store, the pool, the park—I was afraid that something terrible might happen. I was truly scared. Even thirty-minute time-outs weren't cutting it anymore. And, to be honest, I was kind of angry and frustrated, too. I didn't know what kind of discipline I could apply or what kind of positive reinforcement I could use on Katie to keep her safe and sound. Machiavelli was failing me, and I found myself faced with the big guns, the "nuclear option," when it came to his rules. So I pulled out the most infamous Machiavellian maxim of all, one that is as often quoted as it is misinterpreted: "It is better to be feared than loved."

Now, this might make good sense for a prince. But I balked a bit when considering how it might apply in my life, for the obvious reason that all parents want to be loved by their kids. But we also want them to obey our commands, right? Machiavelli was pretty firm on the matter. His full quote says, "It is best to be both feared and loved, but because it is difficult to unite them in one person, it is much safer to be feared than loved."

That might seem hard-hearted. But we're talking about obedience here, and it certainly wasn't safe for Katie to wander off by herself in the middle of the Fun Zone. Still, this edict seemed a bit extreme. But Machiavelli backs it up by saying that "love is preserved by the link of obligation which, owing to the depravity of man, is broken at every opportunity for their advantage; but fear preserves you by a dread of punishment which never fails."

The same holds true for parents and kids. Because, as

we know, young kids don't obey rules because they love their mommy and daddy. Instead, they become more obedient little people because of their fear of being punished by their parents. It's human nature. So don't fight it, Machiavelli would advise. Embrace it—and make it work for you.

Machiavelli isn't advocating the use of cruelty for its own sake, or celebrating it. He's simply saying that sometimes a leader has to be a meanie to ensure the security of the people. Or, in the words of that immortal Nick Lowe song, "Baby, you gotta be cruel to be kind."

That's logical, I thought, but also risky because I didn't want to be viewed by my kids as cruel. But suddenly, after my meltdown at the Fun Zone, they were eyeing me with a new wariness. It was as if, having finally seen the true depths of my anger when prodded, they were terrified of misbehaving again.

All of them except Katie. She'd been mischievously misbehaving for months at home, but I didn't really understand the scope of the problem at school until Eric and I attended her parent-teacher conference at the neighborhood day care center she was attending.

"We all love Katie here," the director said, smiling sweetly. "She plays really well with the other kids, she's very compassionate, and she's making excellent progress."

"That's great," I sighed with pride and relief.

"But," she added, "we're still having a problem with her escaping from the classroom, which poses a danger to the other kids because the teacher can't leave them alone to chase after her. Which, of course, poses a huge liability to us."

"How many times has she escaped?" I asked.

The director grabbed a thick folder from her desk and pulled out a log. "One hundred and six times this month," she announced.

"A hundred and six times? This month?" Eric and I repeated in disbelief.

She nodded and then dealt the final blow: "Katie can stay enrolled so long as she has a one-on-one aide with her all day. Otherwise, we can't allow her to come back."

"Can't she at least stay until the end of the month?" I asked.

"Only if she has a full-time aide" was her firm response.

"But . . . we already paid," I said desperately.

The director smiled sweetly again. "We'll issue a refund."

"Great," I said to Eric as we headed for his car. "We can't afford a full-time aide and tuition. That'd be forty thousand dollars a year, or more."

"We could put her back in public school," he suggested.

"They won't let us mainstream her," I reminded him. "We already lost that battle. Plus, we agreed we don't want her in that special-ed class. It's a forty-five-minute bus ride each way."

"Then she'll have to stay home with you until we figure out what to do," he said decisively.

"But I have to work."

"So do I," he replied. "And I can't work from home like you do."

Clearly, Katie's misbehavior was much more serious

than I had thought. Disobeying at home was one thing. But while part of the same problem, disobeying her teachers at school and endangering the safety of others was far more alarming. Something had to be done.

But what?

When Eric dropped me off it was three o'clock, which meant that I had two hours to finish my brief, which was due that day, and e-mail it to my boss. Stuck between a rock and hard place, I paid the babysitter, then hurried into the kitchen to make a quick afternoon snack. When I rushed into the family room, I saw Teddy and Trevor watching *SpongeBob SquarePants*, but Katie was nowhere in sight.

"Where's Katie?" I asked sharply.

They shrugged.

I raced to the front door to make sure the safety gate was locked, which, thankfully, it was. The kid was still on the premises, thank god. But, as I stepped back into the dining room, which also serves as my office, I watched in horror from across the room as Katie dumped a full—absolutely full—bottle of water on my laptop.

"*No!! Katie!*" I screamed, as my stress level skyrocketed. My brief. My computer. My job.

I'd barely had time to process this catastrophe when Teddy came racing up behind me with a terrible look on her face. "Mom!" she screamed, her eyes flashing with anger and frustration. "Katie tore up my homework! And I can't find Special Kitty!"

"She has to be here somewhere," I assured Teddy, sending her back to her room to search. Then I led Katie into her bedroom and threw down the gauntlet.

"You *cannot* destroy things!" I shouted. "You *cannot* take other people's belongings! And you *cannot* run out of your classroom! You have to *listen* and *obey*!"

Katie looked up at me, frightened and confused.

"You're getting an *hour* time-out this time!" I continued on my tirade. "With *no* toys! And *no* TV! And *no* DVDs!"

"Mom, I still can't find Special Kitty," Teddy pleaded from the next room.

"We'll find her," I said as my anger quickly turned to shame.

"What if Katie took her to school and left her there?" she asked. "Or what if she threw her in the trash?"

And with that, we ran outside and onto our driveway, where three black trash cans stood ominously at the curb. I could see the trash truck driving away in the distance as Teddy raced to the bins and looked inside.

"They're empty!" she sobbed. "She's gone! Special Kitty is gone!"

We stood there in silence for a while. Then Teddy wiped her eyes, looked at me sadly, and asked, "Can I stay with Dad this weekend?"

All of a sudden, I stopped and looked at myself. I couldn't provide Teddy with the peaceful, well-ordered home that she so desperately wanted and needed, and my poor, sweet, infuriating Katie had every right to both fear and hate me. And, at that moment, I hated myself.

My Machiavellian experiment—and my entire life as a mother—had taken a terrible turn for the worse. For whatever reason, Machiavelli's maxim that "it is better to be feared than loved" wasn't working with Katie—and, as a result, my inability to control or even redirect her increasingly destructive and dangerous behavior was tearing my whole family apart.

XIV

A Prince Must Be Deceitful If It Is to His Advantage:
Knowing When (and When Not) to Lie

houghts other than those of Machiavelli spoke to me at that particular dark point in my life. *When it rains, it pours. Things fall apart; the center cannot hold. If life's a bowl of cherries, what am I doing in the pits?* And my own personal favorite: comedienne Lily Tomlin's wry but apt admonishment that *things are gonna get a lot worse before they get worse.*

Still, with some glaring exceptions, I've always been more of an optimist than a pessimist, and, if anything, I'm not a quitter. So I stayed on course, dug a bit deeper into *The Prince*, and I found something that I thought I could work with. All this time, I'd been viewing Machiavelli through rose-colored glasses. He isn't so harsh. His more

sinister statements have been misinterpreted by later readers. And *The Prince* was maybe just one big gag anyway.

But perhaps I had it all wrong. Perhaps Machiavelli was
just as selfish, dark, and devious as his harshest critics suggest. And maybe I needed to embrace some of that spirit
to succeed. With these unsettling thoughts in my mind,
I came to that passage in *The Prince* where Machiavelli asks
whether it is better to be honest or deceitful. On this, he
says that being honest is wise to a certain degree. But to be
successful, a leader should not honor his promises if doing
so will threaten his rule. And, he adds, since all men are dishonest, "a prince must be deceitful if it is to his advantage."

Now, while I agreed that this might work in the political arena, I had always balked at straight-out lying to my
kids. I wasn't sure that this maxim would be so wise to
apply at home. Should parents be deceitful if it's to their
advantage? Is honesty *always* the best policy when it comes
to raising our kids? We all know that children occasionally
lie for a variety of reasons—to get out of trouble, to get
what they want, to impress their friends. But is it ever okay,
I wondered, for parents to deliberately deceive their kids?

And I'm not talking about little white lies like "You're
a great gymnast!" when they can't even do a cartwheel. Or
"The babysitter's here so Mommy and Daddy can run some
errands," when, in fact, Mommy and Daddy desperately
need a quiet dinner alone together and some really stiff
drinks to help repair their marriage and salvage what remains of their sanity.

I'm talking about the really big things in life.

I wasn't sure until a few days after the Fun Zone disaster. It was a Sunday evening. Teddy had just returned from a father-daughter Indian Princess retreat in San Diego, and she looked tired. I was tired, too. So I helped her get her schoolwork ready for the next day, and then she read on her Kindle in the family room (at least one of my Machiavellian lessons had stuck) as I began making dinner.

At some point, Teddy went upstairs to put on her pajamas, and when she went back into the family room she let out a terrible primal scream.

"*Noooo! Katieeee!*" she howled. I sighed. It was happening again. And as I rushed in to see what was happening, I saw Katie tearing pages out of Teddy's school library book.

"You're getting an *hour* time-out!!" Teddy screamed, clearly mimicking me.

"Teddy!" I shouted.

"With *no* toys!!" she continued.

"Stop, Teddy!" I pleaded.

"And *no* TV!!"

"Teddy!" I repeated.

"And *no* DVDs!!"

Then she stormed off to her bedroom in a fury. I grabbed the book from out of Katie's hands, then ran upstairs and knocked softly on Teddy's locked door.

"Open the door, please," I said gently.

"Go away!" she shouted.

"Please, just open the door."

"No! I want to be alone!"

And as much as I wanted to intervene, I knew she had a right to be upset and needed some time to calm down, so I headed back down to the family room.

"You know you're not supposed to do that," I said firmly to Katie.

She giggled innocently and nodded.

"Then you are getting a time-out right after dinner."

When she and Trevor began eating, I went to the master bedroom to catch my breath and check on Blackie and her kittens, which were just beginning to walk. And when I looked in the box, I saw Mucho Macho Man and Smokey vigorously nursing but I didn't see Orange Guy. I searched the closet, in the bathroom, under the bed. He wasn't there. So I rushed back to the closet, and, as I gently lifted Blackie, I saw the tiny lifeless orange kitten lying beneath her. Seeing her dead kitten, Blackie began licking him.

No! I thought. This can't happen!

But it had.

Blackie had accidentally suffocated her tiny kitten.

Not knowing what to do, I just sat there quietly crying as Blackie tried to revive Orange Guy. What am I going to tell my kids? I thought. They'll be crushed. And as much as I didn't want to deceive them, I didn't want their first experience with the birth of a pet to be tied so closely with death.

When Teddy came downstairs the next morning, she shot an angry look at Katie, then looked at me and said, "I can't go to the library today if I don't return my book."

"I'll tell the librarian what happened," I assured her. "And I'll replace it, so don't worry about that."

"Okay," she said softly. "Can I go see the kittens?"

The moment of truth—or deception—had arrived.

"No, honey," I replied. "They're sleeping. But you can see them after school."

"Please," she begged. "I really want to see them. Just for a second?"

"Sorry, honey," I said, glancing at the clock. "And besides, we're already late."

As we drove home from school that day, I knew she'd be eager to see the kittens, so I broached the topic. "So, you know how Orange Guy is the littlest one?" I asked.

"Yeah, the runt," she smiled.

"Yeah . . . well . . . he wasn't getting enough milk so I had to take him to the vet today so they can try to feed him."

Tears welled up in her eyes. "Is he gonna be okay?"

"I hope so."

"How long does he have to be there?" she asked.

"I don't know, honey," I lied. "I'll call the vet tomorrow."

As soon as we got home, Teddy raced upstairs and began petting Blackie. "How come she wasn't feeding him?" she asked.

"She was trying," I sighed. "But it's her first litter and sometimes when you're a new mommy . . . or even an experienced mommy . . . you don't always know what to do."

"Do you think she's worried about him?"

"I'm sure she is," I said. "All mommies worry about their babies."

"I'm worried, too," she whispered. Then she kissed Blackie gently on the head and said, "Don't worry, Blackie. Everything's gonna be okay."

And with that my stomach clenched up in knots again because not only had I deliberately deceived my daughter, I had given her a false sense of hope. But there was no changing course. The words had already been spoken.

Late that night, I called my mom. "The orange kitten died," I spoke softly into the phone.

"Did you tell Teddy?"

"No," I confessed. "I said he wasn't getting enough milk and I'd had to take him to the vet."

And with that I turned around and saw Teddy standing behind me with tears streaming down her confused, grief-stricken face.

"Orange Guy died?" she asked.

I shut the phone as she backed away from me. "Yes, honey, I—"

"You said he wasn't eating . . ."

"I know, honey—"

"You said you took him to the vet . . ."

"Yes, honey, I—"

"You said he might be all right. But you lied."

And she was right. I had deliberately deceived my daughter. And she'd found out, in the most devastating way possible. Note to parents: if you do decide to mislead your children, at least be a little smarter about it than I was.

The next day after school, Teddy went to my mom's house for dinner, as she often does. When she came home, I tried to atone for my sin. We were sitting next to each other watching Blackie gently clean her two surviving kittens.

"I feel so bad for Orange Guy," Teddy said. "Why'd he have to die?"

"I wish I knew the answer to that," I said. "But I don't. All I know is that sometimes kittens die because they're not healthy and sometimes their mommies help them die because they know they won't survive, which gives more milk to the healthy ones. It's very, very sad. But sometimes pets die. It's a part of life. Make sense?"

She nodded but didn't say anything.

"And I'm sorry I didn't tell you the truth," I added. "I just didn't want you to be sad and was trying to protect you. Does that make sense?"

"Yeah," she whispered. "I guess."

In the end, the question of whether honesty is always the best policy when it comes to raising our kids is one that parents must decide for themselves, based on their own personal value systems and their own equally legitimate parental ends. As for me: it was a hard lesson learned. This was one Machiavellian maxim that had, I have to say it, failed me. And worse, I'd failed my daughter. Just a few months earlier, I'd spent so much time teaching her that "George Washington and the Cherry Tree" story, explaining that honesty is one of the most important virtues a person can have. Yet, here I was being dishonest right to her face—and she caught me at it. Which was bad enough, but it also made me a hypocrite, someone who wasn't perhaps fully deserving of her trust.

And while I agreed to some degree that it's sometimes okay for leaders to deceive their people and for parents to tell little white lies to their kids, I also believed that when it comes to the really big things in life we would be well advised to always try to be honest with our kids, or we will run the risk of their emulating our behavior. "If Mommy and Daddy lie to me," they might reason, "why can't I lie to them?"

Equally dangerous, they might begin to lose their trust in us. And if I knew anything from Machiavelli, it was that once a leader loses the trust of his subjects . . . he's doomed.

XV

Internal Subversion Is More Perilous Than External Attacks:
Dealing with Dissent

With the last few hard lessons learned—being feared by my kids and deceiving them were Machiavellian tactics that had both pretty much backfired on me when I'd tried to apply them to my family—I was tempted to toss *The Prince* into the shredder. But something stopped me from pulling the plug on this experiment. For one thing, I didn't have another strategy. For better or for worse, I'm also very competitive and determined (read: stubborn) and, like Richard Nixon (a modern-day politician, by the way, whose character and career provide a prime example of the many uses and abuses of Machiavellian power politics), I found that the thought of failure went against every instinct in my body. In other words, like Julius Caesar crossing the Rubicon, I was in too deep and determined to make this plan succeed.

It actually had worked pretty well on some issues. Machiavelli's maxim that "he who wishes to be obeyed must know how to command" had helped me empower myself as a parent. His insight that "the more sand that passes through the hourglass of life the more clearly we see through it" had given me perspective and was helping me enjoy the time that I had with my kids instead of squandering it. And his edict that "a leader must maintain the respect of his subjects" had helped me wage a (mostly) successful battle against back talk.

Yet, as I kept applying Machiavellian tactics to maintain order in our home, ever more audible grumblings of discontent would invariably ensue. In addition to Katie's increasingly challenging behaviors, which had a direct impact on all of us, Teddy was carrying some lingering discontent about how I had handled the death of Orange Guy. And Daniel, it seemed, hadn't yet fully forgotten my earlier disciplining attempts with him.

I knew from *The Prince* that domestic dissent and wavering of will were to be expected at times in any state, no matter how just or well planned a leader's rule. But I also knew that internal subversion is the most dangerous consequence of a leader losing the trust of his subjects. "Internal subversion is more perilous than external attacks," Machiavelli warns, "and if a prince doesn't take care to avoid the hatred of the people, he will live in a state of constant fear."

State of constant fear?

I could relate to that. But what is a prince (or a parent) to do when their subjects (or kids) lose trust in them and rebel?

Machiavelli answers by saying that a leader must crush internal subversion before it gains sufficient momentum to threaten his rule. Toward that end, some princes disarmed the citizenry, some divided towns, some tried to win over disloyal subjects, and some built fortresses to prevent rebellions or destroyed them to maintain control of a newly acquired state. But Machiavelli goes out of his way to say that the success of any particular strategy depends on the circumstances and that few "final judgments" can be made. What he is willing to firmly say, however, is that "princes become great when they overcome the difficulties and obstacles by which they are confronted."

So, to overcome any grumblings of discontent in my home, I had to nip internal subversion in the bud and defeat opposition in whatever form it took, even if it was my own rebellious and subversive young subject. But that's not always easy to do, Machiavelli cautions, because directly related to domestic insurrections are conspiracies. And he should know, because not only was he imprisoned and tortured for his alleged role in a failed conspiracy to assassinate a Medici prince, but one of the bloodiest upheavals in Renaissance Florence—the Pazzi conspiracy—occurred when Machiavelli was nine years old.

This, briefly, is what happened:

On Easter Sunday in 1478, during High Mass in the Cathedral of Florence, assassins, armed with daggers, attacked Lorenzo de' Medici and his brother Giuliano in an attempt to overthrow the government. Stabbed through the chest, Giuliano took a few steps, then fell and bled to death on the cathedral floor, while two armed priests came up behind Lorenzo, who defended himself with his own weapon and fled to the sacristy.

As word of the assassination spread, enraged Florentines seized and killed the conspirators. Plotters were hanged, beheaded, or thrown out of palace windows alive and hacked to pieces in the streets. Meanwhile, each of the bodies of the three main conspirators—a leading member of the rival Pazzi family and the archbishop of Pisa, among them—were left dangling for days above the Piazza della Signoria.

"All the city was up in arms," an observer wrote, "all over the city the name of the Medici was shouted, and the limbs of the dead were seen either stuck on the points of weapons or dragged through the city, and everybody with words full of anger and deeds full of cruelty hunted down the Pazzi."

Was the young Niccolò an eyewitness to these dreadful acts? Or, as historian Sebastian De Grazia asks, "Was he quickly shunted behind closed, bolted doors?" No one knows. But he lived with his family only a few miles from the carnage, and "the sight of bodies being torn apart by angry crowds" or stories he heard later of these "grave and tumultuous events" must have left a mark on the mind of the young Machiavelli, whose pessimistic view of human nature was forged, according to one biographer, "when his peaceful childhood was violently shattered."

And as I thought about this, I wondered if maybe Machiavelli's own turbulent life—and the turbulent times in which he lived—was what had, in fact, largely shaped his political philosophy. Maybe because he knew that men were capable of such depraved behavior, he figured that swift and severe punishment dispensed with an iron fist was what was needed when the going got tough. Whatever the case, I did agree that both princes and parents must crush internal subversion before it gains sufficient momentum to threaten their rule. Unfortunately, I lacked the virtù to rise to the occasion and suffered one of my greatest defeats one Sunday afternoon when Eric went off to his office and I stayed home with Trevor and Katie and tried to finish a brief.

Thankfully, Trevor was napping in the family room, so I tucked him under a blanket and gave a bowl of sliced oranges to Katie, who was sitting happily beside him. I put my laptop (newly replaced after the recent water-dumping incident) right behind them and began writing. After a few minutes, Katie stood up and pointed upstairs, indicating that she wanted to nap in her own room, as she often likes to do. So I walked her upstairs, tucked her in bed, and continued writing for a half hour, until three loud pounds on the front door shattered the rare midafternoon silence.

What happened in the moments that followed is still so vivid to me that it plays out in my mind like a movie:

FADE IN.

INTERIOR. EVANS-WOODS RESIDENCE. DAY

Suzy opens the front door and from her point of view we see two male POLICE OFFICERS, one mid-40s, the other late 20s. A female POLICE OFFICER, early 30s, stands behind them, glaring angrily at Suzy.

OLDER POLICE OFFICER (to Suzy): Do you have a daughter about five years old? Down syndrome?

SUZY (confused): Yes, Katie.

OLDER POLICE OFFICER: She's all right. She's in one of our vehicles outside.

SUZY: What?!

OLDER POLICE OFFICER: One of your neighbors found her walking along the street about ten houses from here.

SUZY: Oh my god . . .

Now she knows what happened.

SUZY (CONT'D): My husband must've forgotten to lock the safety gate when he left.

FEMALE POLICE OFFICER (angrily): Hey, don't blame anyone else here. This is your responsibility.

OLDER POLICE OFFICER: Where's your husband?

SUZY: At work. He left about a half hour ago, and we always lock this gate so she can't escape.

OLDER POLICE OFFICER: Has she done this before?

A pause.

SUZY: Yes . . . she's been kicked out of two schools this year because she escapes all the time. She . . . thinks it's a game.

FEMALE POLICE OFFICER: Has she escaped from home before?

SUZY: Once. About six months ago when my husband was here.

OLDER POLICE OFFICER: You know we could arrest you for child neglect and endangerment?

Suzy nods, terrified and visibly shaking.

OLDER POLICE OFFICER (CONT'D): Do you have other kids?

SUZY: Yes . . .

OLDER POLICE OFFICER: How many?

SUZY: A daughter. A son. And a stepson.

He takes notes.

OLDER POLICE OFFICER: How old are they?

SUZY: Uh . . . nine, eight, and three.

More notes.

FEMALE POLICE OFFICER: You know if we
called Child Protective Services you could lose all
of your kids.

A long pause as this terrible reality sinks in.

OLDER POLICE OFFICER (CONT'D): And if
Katie does this again and gets hurt, you could go
to prison for a very long time.

*Now everything's at stake—her family, her freedom, her
home, her kids. Barely able to speak, Suzy nods as the older
officer's cell phone rings. He talks into it for a few seconds,
then closes it.*

OLDER POLICE OFFICER: What's your husband's
name?

SUZY: Eric Woods.

He writes it down.

FEMALE POLICE OFFICER: You know she escapes. How did this happen?

SUZY: I assumed my husband locked the gate, so
I took her upstairs to nap but she must've waited
until I wasn't looking and snuck out. . . . I thought
she was in her room.

More notes.

OLDER POLICE OFFICER: Why don't you tell me
some things you can do to make sure this never
happens again.

SUZY: I'll put an alarm on the door.

FEMALE POLICE OFFICER: You should've done
that before.

Suzy nods.

SUZY: And I'll put bells and extra locks on all the
windows and doors.

OLDER POLICE OFFICER (reaching for his hand-
cuffs): Can I step inside for a minute?

SUZY (terrified): Sure . . .

He steps inside and looks around. Trevor's on the couch staring at them with his thumb in his mouth. Blackie's watching the whole scene from the stairs.

OLDER POLICE OFFICER (stepping outside): I'm allergic to cats.

SUZY: We've got two kittens, too.

A long, terrible silence.

OLDER POLICE OFFICER: All right, I'm going to file a report and hopefully you won't ever have to see us again. But you promise me that if we come back next week, all of these things will be done. The locks, the alarms?

SUZY: Yes . . .

The female officer glares at her.

OLDER POLICE OFFICER: Okay, your daughter's in a vehicle on the street.

EXTERIOR. STREET. MOMENTS LATER.

Katie emerges from a police car, giggling and smiling like she's been having a fabulous time. The older officer hands Suzy some forms to sign; then all three officers get in separate cars and, one by one, pull away from the curb and drive off, leaving Suzy standing alone in the driveway with Katie.

FADE OUT.

In exile, facing financial ruin, and struggling to support his young family, Machiavelli wrote to his friend Francesco Vettori. "I don't know how much longer I can continue on this way," he complained, "until I become contemptible because of my poverty." His oppressed spirits also found voice in a note he wrote in the margins of a document he was working on at the time: *post res perditas—after everything was lost.*

Like Machiavelli, I realized that I, too, now faced the very real possibility of losing everything that mattered most to me. I was losing the trust and support of my family fast—and what's more, I was starting not to trust myself. What if I just couldn't do this? Was raising a child with Katie's kind of special needs just too much for me?

In *The Prince*, Machiavelli admonishes that "the unarmed prophets" always come to ruin. At that moment I, too, felt totally defenseless—or unarmed—as a parent. Katie and the challenges I faced raising her were overwhelming me. And I felt sure that one false move, one moment of distraction, would lead to total ruin.

Not knowing what to do or whom to turn to, I referred in desperation again to *The Prince* and came to that point where Machiavelli shifts his emphasis from dispensing concrete advice to describing the personality traits of a successful prince, some of which, I learned, are more critical than others. Building on this, he reiterates—as if to mock me, I thought—that a prince must avoid being hated by his people and then draws a distinction between appearing virtuous and actually being virtuous. Displaying such virtuous traits as benevolence is desirable, he says, but not necessary, whereas appearing virtuous is crucial. He clarifies this by saying that traits such as decisiveness are more useful than generosity because liberality leads to poverty, as we have seen, whereas decisiveness breeds respect and prestige.

And this is where Machiavelli offers a critical tip, because he says that a prince becomes respected by decisively striking an alliance on one side of a conflict or another. "A prince is respected," Machiavelli advises, "when without any reservation he declares himself in favor of one party against the other."

This, he says, will always be safer "than standing neutral because if two of your powerful neighbors come to blows, they are of such a character that, if one of them conquers, you have either to fear him or not." But if you do not declare yourself "you will invariably fall prey to the conqueror and you will not have anything to protect or shelter you." Why? Because "he who conquers does not want doubtful friends who will not aid him in the time of trial, and he who loses will not harbor you because you did not willingly, sword in hand, court his fate."

Like an embattled prince, with sword in hand, courting my fate, I was in desperate need of an ally. But there was one little glitch, which was that Eric and I, who should have been the strongest and most loyal of allies in times of crisis, had major differences of opinion over how to address Katie's increasingly dangerous behaviors, ones that I now feared posed a grave risk of harm to herself and others.

Eric, however, didn't share my fears, and when he returned home shortly after the police officers departed, it was clear that he didn't understand the gravity of the situation.

"You forgot to lock the safety gate and I was the one who was almost arrested," I said with my heart still racing.

"I'm sorry," he said. "But you've forgotten to lock it before."

"That's not the point!" I said sharply. "And if it happens again, we'll both go to jail and lose all of our kids!"

"You should've watched her more carefully," he said flatly.

Now I was freaking out and furious. "You have no idea what it's like staying home all day with a child who doesn't listen to *anything* you say! Who destroys *everything* you have and laughs! Who's five years old and hasn't said *Mommy* yet!" I paused, then added, "Maybe things would be easier if she could just talk."

"Easier for who?" he asked.

We glared at each other, like two princes locked in battle.

"And you're right," he added. "I don't know what it's like. But why don't you try looking at it for once from her perspective? Maybe she escaped because she was trying to get a reaction from you. Negative attention's better than no attention."

"No attention? She takes up all of my time so I can't focus on anyone or anything else!"

"That's your problem," he said. "You've always been selfish with your time. And you're always so wrapped up in your own little world that you can't see—"

"My own little world?" I repeated. "I don't do *anything* for myself! All I do is take care of other people's needs!"

"And how's that working?"

And with that, I stormed off in a fury.

But . . . I had nowhere to go. I felt totally lost, overwhelmed, and alone. I loved my little Katie-Girl, but dealing with her was so hard and my inability to assert my power over her was tearing my family apart. Nothing was working. No matter how hard I had tried, I couldn't meet her many special needs. And even though a five-star general probably couldn't have gotten her to fall into line, I felt that I was failing catastrophically as a mother. I was fearful, indecisive, and weak—the exact opposite of the virtù that Machiavelli espouses.

Worse, I was showing that weakness to my family, and it was crumbling. My husband and I weren't working together as allies. We were working against each other like open enemies, partly because I had lashed out at him in my own anger and frustration. Even worse, my kids were losing their faith in me. Seeing me freaking out, they were scared, too—all of which made me feel absolutely awful. I was desperate and at the end of my rope. Not only had I lost all perspective, I was terrified that I was on the verge of losing my whole family.

Desperate for help, I called an old friend and let everything out. Having four kids of her own, and well aware of my many struggles with Katie, she understood the depth of my desperation and, after I managed to calm down a bit, she suggested the possibility of adoption. "It's too hard," she offered. "You've tried your best. And no one will blame you."

After I hung up, I called my mom and told her what had happened. Worried and wanting to protect her own daughter, she offered her thoughts, then told me to call my father for guidance. He, too, listened intently, then, with a soft but firm voice, said, "You can't do it anymore, Suzy. You can't watch her every split second of the day. Eric could forget to lock the gate again, or you could, and you *will* lose everything. You have to think of your other kids."

"There are group homes she'd be happy in," I heard my stepmother, Kris, offer in the background.

"Did you tell your mom?" my dad asked.

"Yeah."

"What'd she say?"

I paused, then whispered, "The same thing."

When I hung up, I wondered if maybe they were right. Maybe Katie did deserve a better mother, one who could consistently meet her many needs, something that I was clearly unable to do. Overwhelmed with guilt and shame, I went on the Internet and typed into Google "Down Syndrome Adoption" and clicked on the top link.

Was this the ally I needed?

More important, was this the ally Katie needed?

PART III

Finding My Way Home

"Midway on our life's journey," Machiavelli's literary hero Dante writes in *The Inferno*, "I found myself in dark woods, the right road lost." Midway on my own life's journey, I, too, found myself at my darkest hour, the right road lost. Desperate, fearful, and lonely, I thought about my family's future and then back to Katie and her first days with me, another dark and difficult time in my life that I'm not particularly proud of but that proves the truth of Machiavelli's most revealing insights on human nature . . . insights that helped me finally find my way home.

XVI

There Are Only Individual Egos Crazy for Love:
Overcoming Your Deepest Fears

ewind nearly six years. It was the Friday before Mother's Day in 2005. Twelve weeks pregnant, I was out casually shopping for a new (read: bigger) pair of jeans. And I received a phone call from my ob-gyn's assistant, who informed me that the results of my first trimester prenatal screening test had come back with a statistical risk of 1:3 that the fetus I was carrying had Down syndrome.

Based on my age at the time, the risk should have been about 1:180. I was terrified by the results, but tried not to worry too much, assuring myself with the fact that the test has a notoriously high rate of false positives. Still, I had to decide whether to have an amniocentesis, a minimally invasive prenatal test that carries a 1:200 risk of miscarriage but gives a definitive diagnosis.

For more than a month, I struggled with the decision, terrified of the possibility of miscarriage. Yet, at the same time, I had this deep maternal instinct that my baby did have Down syndrome. Something about this pregnancy just felt different than my previous one, which made the decision much more difficult because I knew that if I opted to not take the test, and my baby did have Down syndrome, I would be depriving myself of critical medical information upon which to base the next parental decision: whether to have an abortion.

For the next eight weeks, I read everything I could find on Down syndrome. I scoured the Internet. I devoured books, blogs, and medical journals. And most of what I learned was disturbing: that Down syndrome is associated with all sorts of medical problems and varying degrees of mental retardation, from moderate to profound. I also found studies that showed that about 95 percent of American women who learn that they're carrying a fetus with Down syndrome choose to terminate the pregnancy.

This statistic raised a whole new set of fears: Why are so many people afraid of Down syndrome? Do the presumed burdens and defects associated with the syndrome almost always justify abortion? And if my baby does have Down syndrome and I choose not to have an abortion, will I be viewed by society with prejudice, pity, or even scorn?

"Why didn't she just have an abortion," some people might say disapprovingly.

Beginning in week 20, I began to feel my baby kick and finally decided not to have an amniocentesis for the simple if selfish reason that I didn't want to put myself in the position of playing God and making a decision that I knew I would regret for the rest of my life, regardless of how devastating the alternative might be or what burdens it might place on my family and me.

At that point, I let go of my fears and, for the remainder of my pregnancy, tried hard not to think about the "what-ifs." I relaxed even more as each bimonthly ultrasound didn't reveal any markers for Down syndrome, and, as the last weeks of my pregnancy slowly progressed, I began to feel more and more confident that the screening test had, in fact, been inaccurate.

All of this anxiety will be forgotten as soon as I see my baby, I assured myself.

On November 15, 2005, I went in for my week 37 ultrasound. By then, the appointments had become routine. But when the sonographer fell silent and suddenly left the room without saying a word, a wave of worry washed over me.

Moments later, the perinatologist entered the room, silently studied the grainy black screen, then said matter-of-factly, "Your amniotic fluid is dangerously low. You're gonna have this baby today. Go straight to Labor and Delivery and I will call your doctor." Then he exited the room as quietly and unceremoniously as he had entered.

What? I thought, in denial and shock. I'm not ready to have this baby. My bag isn't packed. I have work to do. And I have to pick up my daughter at three o'clock!

As I got dressed in a daze, I glanced at the screen and saw that my baby's long bones (the femur and humerus) were measuring at thirty-three weeks. But I was in my thirty-seventh week! That was four weeks behind! It was then that all of my fears about Down syndrome came rushing back over me. From months of obsessive research, I knew that "shortened long bones" was a strong physiological sign of Down syndrome.

As I headed toward the hospital, I thought, Today will either be one of the happiest days of my life or one of the most devastating, and I will know which one in a few hours. This sense of finality lent some relief to an otherwise terrifying situation. There would be no more tests to take, no more weeks left to worry about things I couldn't control. My baby would soon be born, whether or not she had Down syndrome.

Eric arrived in the operating room a few minutes after the epidural was administered. After the blue screen was put up, I felt a few tugs, then saw our baby being lifted up and her umbilical cord cut.

As Katie let out her first cries of life, Eric excitedly grabbed his camera and began snapping photographs.

"Is she okay?" I asked, afraid of the answer.

"She's beautiful!" he exclaimed, clicking more pictures.

Maybe she is okay, I thought, and, for a moment, my maternal spirit soared. But my hopes were shattered when I heard the neonatologist whisper, "Did she have an amnio?"

"No," my obstetrician quietly replied.

Why would she ask that? I panicked. No one had asked

that when my first daughter was born. But nothing else was said. My doctor stitched me back up, congratulated me, and then quietly slipped out of the room.

More than an hour passed, and no one said anything about Down syndrome. But still, I was filled with a sense of doom. Then a nurse brought Katie to us, swaddled tightly in a pink flannel blanket and tiny white hospital cap.

As Eric gently cradled her in his arms, I studied her face with clinical detachment. Her eyes slanted upward, her tongue occasionally thrust out as if it was too large for her mouth, and her face looked somewhat flattened. But still, no one said anything. The nurse sat with us for another hour, chatting about trivial matters and laughing casually with the hospital staff. I just lay there, silently shaking, waiting for the other shoe to drop.

When the sky outside began to darken, the neonatologist entered the room. She had dark brown skin and darker brown eyes, and she glided silently across the room like a shadow. To me, she looked like the Grim Reaper. When she reached the edge of my hospital bed, she looked down at me for a moment, then uttered that one simple sentence that changed my life forever: "Your baby shows signs of Down syndrome."

And that was it.

The words had finally been spoken.

As I watched the Grim Reaper's mouth move, spewing out words like "possible heart defects" and "mental retardation," I looked at Eric and literally saw the color drain from his face, a face that, just a few moments earlier, had been flush with happiness and pride and excitement about our new family life. But now he just sat there, silently processing this devastating information.

When the Grim Reaper stopped talking, I heard Eric quietly say, "Okay." Then I turned my face toward the wall and felt a single warm tear slowly roll down my right cheek.

After that, everything got blurry and I felt as if I were watching myself in a movie. I could see myself from a distance, lying in the hospital bed. I could see the Grim Reaper standing next to me. This is not my life, I thought. This is not happening to me. It's happening to another version of me.

I later learned that this phenomenon is a psychological defense mechanism that the brain employs to dissociate itself from situations too traumatic or devastating to immediately process or accept. It's as if the psyche temporarily disassociates itself from itself—hence the feeling of being outside of oneself, watching oneself.

I will never forget that moment because, in that moment, everything in my life changed. Before Katie was born, I'd led what I felt was a very charmed life. But now, it seemed, tragedy had struck. My luck had finally run out.

As I lay in the recovery room not wanting to look at or hold my baby, I felt as if my world was falling apart. My life, as I had known it, was over. How would this affect Teddy? What would it do to my relationship with Eric? And how would I cope?

When I finally looked at my baby, I was overwhelmed by intense feelings of grief, fear, revulsion, and shock. And when Eric asked if I wanted to hold her, I shook my head and quietly said that I couldn't because my body was still shaking too hard from the epidural. But that wasn't true, and I knew it. I just didn't want to hold her. Holding her would make her real. Holding her would make her mine. And I didn't want her to be mine.

After a few hours, the reality began to sink in, and I knew that we had to tell our family and friends that our baby might have Down syndrome. I also knew that I couldn't say those words without sobbing, so Eric called my parents for me.

My father, a very wise and rational man, was silent for a while, then, with a quavering voice, gently said, "It doesn't matter."

My mother, in denial, quickly offered, "Maybe the doctor is wrong."

Most people, however, simply said, "I'm sorry," which are the most painful words of all to hear when you have just had a baby.

Thankfully, Katie passed all of her medical tests and so, three long days after she was born, she and I were released from the hospital and I went home with a baby I did not want. I wanted a baby, just not this particular baby.

I am, of course, very ashamed to admit this. But that's the truth. That's exactly how I felt. And I have since learned that this is how some parents of babies with Down syndrome and other serious congenital anomalies feel in the first few days and weeks immediately following the birth, especially if they didn't learn of their baby's condition prenatally.

For me, the first few months of Katie's life were agonizing. I did not bond with her. I did not feel love for her. And I cried all the time, especially in the middle of the night when I was breast-feeding her or changing her diapers, because I felt like I was taking care of someone else's baby and because I wished that she were someone else's baby.

Being alone in the house with her was also hard. But going out in public was even worse. Wherever I went—the grocery store, the mall, the park—all I saw were happy young mothers with their beautiful, "normal" babies. Occasionally, a happy young mother would look at Katie and smile uncomfortably, then glance at me with obvious pity and turn away, not knowing what to do or say. Because these social exchanges were so painful, I began covering Katie's stroller with a blanket so no one could see her.

Then, when Katie was three months old, something happened to her that changed me forever as her parent. She contracted Hib (*Haemophilus influenzae* type b) disease, a rare form of bacterial meningitis that, before the advent of vaccines, was deadly in about one out of every ten cases. We rushed her to our pediatrician, who told us to go straight to the Children's Hospital, where she was immediately taken from my arms and rushed to the pediatric intensive care unit to be given a spinal tap.

The next morning, the pediatric infectious disease specialist told us that intravenous antibiotics might cure the infection, if we had caught it in time, but they wouldn't know for seventy-two hours. And so I spent the next three days and nights sitting in that hospital room, terrified that my baby, who I thought I did not want, might die.

As terrifying as that week was, it was also profoundly

transformative because it was then that I finally stopped crying for myself. The tears that I shed were no longer for me. They were for Katie—because here was this beautiful three-month-old baby girl, who had just had a spinal tap, was battling a deadly infection, and was hooked up to an IV for a week, but still woke up every morning smiling.

From that week on, I began to see Katie for who she is: a precious little girl. Like other little girls, she gets cranky when she's hungry or tired, likes pizza and chocolate chip cookies, and loves to splash in the bath. For too long, all I saw when I looked at my daughter was her diagnosis. But what I was now finally able to see was my beautiful little girl.

My daughter was born with Down syndrome.

What made that hard fact even more devastating (for both of us) was that I didn't know if I could or would grow to love her. But after the shock wore off, I saw that my love for her had always been there. It was just buried deep beneath my initial sorrow and grief. And while raising Katie is probably the most difficult thing I will ever do, she is my daughter and I will never, ever, ever give her up.

Machiavelli, of course, is not so well known for his insights on love. But, looking back, I could see that one of his maxims did have great resonance to my life at that time, which was this: when stripped of power struggles and endless conflict "there are only individual egos crazy for love." And the most crazy and unwavering love you'll ever find is between parent and child.

Yes, life can be hard and full of heartbreak at times. Friends, jobs, houses, and even spouses may come and go.

But the one bond of love and obligation that never fails is the one between parent and child, even, and especially, in times of great turmoil and crisis.

For all that Machiavelli can teach us about princes and power and politics, he can, it seems, teach us even more about human nature and who we—as individuals, as families, and as a society—truly are. And when it comes to the sometimes hard realities of parenting, that kind of knowledge, I thought, can be the most empowering, enlightening, and transformative knowledge of all. And something tells me that Machiavelli would agree with me on this.

XVII

Recognize the Capable and Keep Them Faithful:
Finding and Keeping Allies

I am, of course, deeply ashamed to admit that I even considered such an extreme option as giving up my beautiful Katie. It was my darkest hour, my most humbling moment as a mother . . . and my most revealing truth. But what it made me see was that I needed help—more help, perhaps, than I'd been having; maybe more help than the tough-minded Machiavelli could provide me with. What I needed to figure out was how to ask for and receive help.

I also knew that this would be more easily said than done, of course. And that's where Machiavelli has some insights that apply here, too, especially in relation to his advice on the relationships between a ruler and his advisers (sometimes he also refers to his "servants"). Without these trusted confidants and helpers, a prince—no matter how powerful, how resourceful, how full of virtù—is unable to administer his government. Yeah, I was starting to understand that.

"The choice of servants is of no little importance to a prince," Machiavelli proclaims, "and they are good or not according to the discrimination of the prince. And the first opinion which one forms of a prince, and of his understanding, is by observing the men he has around him; and when they are capable and faithful he may always be considered wise, because he has known how to recognize the capable and to keep them faithful." But when they are otherwise, he advises, one "cannot form a good opinion of him for the prime error which he made was in choosing them."

Okay. So a prince and a parent should choose their confidants, friends, and advisers carefully. Yes, that's good advice. But how can we ensure that we will make a wise choice? Machiavelli offers this critical tip: "To enable a prince to form an opinion of his servant there is one test which never fails: when you see the servant thinking more of his own interests than of yours, and seeking inwardly his own profit in everything, such a man will never make a good servant, nor will you ever be able to trust him" because "he ought never pay any attention to matters in which the prince is not concerned."

That makes sense, right? But Machiavelli goes further and says that to keep his adviser honest, a prince "ought to study him, honoring him, enriching him, doing him kindnesses," and "at the same time let him see that he cannot stand alone." When servants and princes are thus disposed, he concludes, "they can trust each other, but when it is otherwise, the end will always be disastrous for either one or the other."

Great. But as I thought about this and my own advisers (or seeming lack thereof), I realized that, despite my many recent disagreements with my husband, he has always been there for me, through all of the ups and downs. Our marriage certainly isn't a fairy tale. But, in addition to my parents, Eric is the strongest, closest, and most loyal and loving "ally" I have ever had. When I fell apart after Katie was born, he was there: strong as a rock, willing and able to help us confront and overcome whatever reversals of fortune came our way. He has always believed in me, encouraged me to follow my dreams, and been my greatest confidant and companion. To this extent, then, Machiavelli's insights on the potentially disastrous relationships between a prince and his advisers didn't seem to have much relevance in my life.

But a closer reading made me recoil in horror as I saw in them a reflection of myself more clearly than had I been peering, stark naked, into a full-length, fluorescent-lit department store mirror, one that revealed in terrible spine-chilling detail all of my worst human foibles and flaws, and what I saw was a blinding glimpse of what was preventing me from being the kind of mother that I had always longed to be, the kind of mother that my children, especially Katie, so desperately wanted and needed.

Reasoning loosely by analogy, it eventually hit me that Machiavelli's insights cut to the very heart of the relationship between not only a prince and his adviser, but between parent and child. Sounds strange, I know. But if you replace "prince" with "child" and substitute "parent" for "servant," Machiavelli's passages would read: to enable a child to form an opinion of his parent there is one test that never fails: when you see the parent putting their own interests above those of their child, such a person will never make a good parent, nor will the child ever be able to trust them, because they ought never pay any attention to matters in which the child is not concerned. And when parent and child are thus disposed, as Machiavelli would caution, the end will always be disastrous for either one or the other.

Had I through all of these long hard years put my own interests, my own personal struggles, above those of Katie?

To his credit, Eric accepted Katie—and her disability—from the day she was born. But unlike him and so many other wonderful mothers and fathers of children with special needs who are quick to accept and embrace the precious gift they have received, I wasn't able to do the same. One reason, however damning, is that for most of my adult life I have valued learning and language, intelligence and achievement to such a degree that it made me see Katie's birth and her mental disabilities as a tragedy, one from which I had not yet fully recovered.

The birth of a child with Down syndrome is not a tragedy. In some ways, it's an incredible if unexpected blessing—one that can knock even the strongest among us to our knees with grief but forever enlarge our understanding of what it means to be fully human. I, of course, wasn't enlightened enough to immediately see this, and on the day that Katie was born it felt as if my heart shattered into a million tiny pieces right there on the delivery room floor. But instead of slowly healing, it began to harden.

The one and perhaps only thing I can say in my defense is that I have always loved her as deeply and completely as my other children. The terrible question I now had to confront, however, was: Did she love me? How could she?

Not easy matters to face privately, let alone openly and honestly, but it was only in facing these realities that I was able to finally forge a new, true beginning in my relationship with Katie, one formed and informed not by Machiavellian notions of power and authority but by a deeper, more transformative understanding of what it means to be not only a mother but a human being.

When I sat next to Katie and held her hand before bedtime that night, she turned her eyes away from me. "So there are a million things I need to say to you," I said softly, "but all that I'll say now is that I love you very much and I'll understand if you're really mad at me, because if I were you, I'd be really mad at me, too." I paused, then added, "We both have a lot of healing to do, but we'll do it together, and I promise I'll do everything I can to make things right. Okay?"

She sat there for a while, then looked up and stared me square in the eye.

A moment of recognition between mother and child.

After a while, she smiled, then wrapped her arms around me and nestled her head against my chest, and for the first time I heard her say clearly with a whisper, "*Mommy*." And as I smiled through my tears, I felt my heart begin to soften and become whole again.

Did she forgive me?

Was this the beginning of my redemption?

I didn't know. But what I did know was that when Machiavelli sat down to write his little masterpiece, he was, as we have seen, in the midst of an intense moment of crisis. What is not so well known, however, is that around the same time, his wife gave birth to a daughter who soon afterward died. The death weighed heavily on Machiavelli, as it would on any parent. "Physically I feel well," he wrote in a letter to his nephew Giovanni in which he referred to his daughter's death, "but ill in every other respect."

I cannot imagine the grief a parent experiences upon the death of a child. And while I would never compare the birth of a child with Down syndrome to such a terrible tragedy, I was in the months and years following Katie's birth grieving the death of the dream of the child that I was planning on having but lost.

The journey out of that abyss hasn't been easy and the pain of it will probably never go away, as Emily Perl Kingsley so poignantly wrote in her poem "Welcome to Holland," in which she compares what it's like to raise a child with Down syndrome to a much-anticipated trip to Italy that gets diverted. And what I learned on my own journey (and from poet Kahlil Gibran) is that "the deeper sorrow carves into your heart the more joy it can contain."

"It is by going down into the abyss that we recover the treasures of life," Joseph Campbell wrote. "Where you stumble, there lies your treasure." I had gone down into the abyss in my journey with Katie. But where I stumbled, there was my treasure.

Like Kingsley and Campbell, Machiavelli also spoke to me on this. Because what I learned is that at the heart of his political philosophy is the notion of contingency—or flexibility. In particular, what Machiavelli saw and stated matter-of-factly but which his predecessors had only tacitly acknowledged, if they saw it at all, is that for men to take the contingencies of history in stride, they must be highly contingent and suit their conduct to the times.

This philosophy also relates to parenting, and applying it in my life gave me the clarity to see that I had been failing catastrophically as a mother due to my inability to effectively respond to the shifting contingencies—or challenges—in my life with Katie. But once I began shaping my behavior to the situations I was contending with (raising a very spirited special-needs child), I was able to take those contingencies in stride and suit my conduct to the times.

In the end, the best (and most important) ally I needed to win over was myself. What I also realized, however ironically, is that the key to my own parental happiness and success—and the happiness and success of my family—didn't hinge so much on trying to shape or change my children's behavior as it did on changing my own behavior. Or, as Machiavelli would advise: not only to succeed but to survive, a leader must rely first and foremost on himself and his own virtù and valor. And that critical bit of advice applies not only to the relationship between a prince and his people but to the relationship between parent and child.

XVIII

Go Straight to the Truth of Things, Rather Than Dwell in Dreams:
Accepting What Is

With this new sense of resolution and purpose, and nearing the end of *The Prince*, I found myself wanting to know more about who Machiavelli was as a man. And what I discovered is that despite his bad rap, he was quite an honorable and upright—if somewhat bawdy and abrasive—guy. And while he did habitually cheat on his wife, as many Florentine men did at the time (not that it makes it right!), he was a loving father, loyal friend, and brutally honest observer of the human condition. He commented on everything he saw—the cruelty, brutality, lies, and deceit, as well as the bravery and brilliance—and wasn't afraid to tell it like it is.

Machiavelli's hardheaded analysis later established him

as the founding father of political science, a field that investigates politics as it is actually practiced as opposed to how some philosophers and idealists might think it ought to be practiced. His commitment to the truth is also at the heart of his originality and is, if not explicitly then implicitly, on each and every page of *The Prince.* We see it in his dedicatory letter to Lorenzo de' Medici where he writes of telling "the effective truth of the matter." We see it in chapter 15 when he says, "It seems best to me to go straight to the actual truth of things, rather than to dwell in dreams." And we see it in chapter 23 where he says that in seeking advice a leader must make it clear that "the truth does not offend him."

And as I thought about this it hit me that these concepts have direct relevance in our lives as modern-day mothers and fathers. And by that I mean that as we go through our days trying to raise our kids to the best of our abilities, shouldn't we "go straight to the actual truth of things rather than to dwell in dreams" (as I had at times, especially with Katie)? And when seeking advice on specific problems that arise with our kids, shouldn't we let it be known that "the truth does not offend" us?

On this, Machiavelli acknowledges that a prince must seek advice, but cautions that he should only ask for it when he wants it, not when others "thrust it upon him." A prince must also always be skeptical of the advice he receives, and should he ever discover that he is being flattered or deceived, he should "let his anger be felt." Courts are full of flatterers, he says, because "men are so self-complacent in their own affairs, and in a way so deceived in them, that a prince is preserved with difficulty from this pest."

What does he mean by this? Well, in speaking of flatter-ers, he is referring, I learned, to those people who deceive a leader by telling him what they think he wants to hear, as opposed to always speaking the truth. On this, he says that in seeking advice, a prince "ought to choose the wise men in his state, and give to them only the liberty of speaking the truth to him, and then only of those things of which he inquires, and of none others; but he ought to question them upon everything, and listen to their opinions, and afterwards form his own conclusions" and "be steadfast in his resolutions." He who does otherwise, he concludes, "will either be overthrown by flatterers or change his mind so often and in so many ways that respect for him abates."

As always, Machiavelli offers an example. This time, it's the Holy Roman emperor Maximilian I, aptly described by one historian as "rash yet timid, obstinate yet fickle, always in a hurry, yet always too late." Maximilian also failed as a leader, Machiavelli says, because he was a "very secretive man" who "consulted with no one, yet never got his own way in anything." He didn't communicate his plans to any-one and, when he tried to carry them out, he was invariably persuaded to change course by flatterers or his advisers. As a result, "those things he did one day he were undone the next, and no one ever understood what he wished or intended to do, and no one could rely on his resolutions." In other words, a ruler is doomed if he can't see the truth for himself, form his own conclusions, and hold firm in his resolutions.

This was standard advice in the many "Mirror of Princes" handbooks (little self-help-like books for new and aspiring rulers) that were circulating around Europe in Machiavelli's day, most of which contained the trite, moralistic advice that a leader must always be virtuous, merciful, benevolent, and kind. For Machiavelli, these platitudes were not only laughable but dangerous, and he exploded them for "preventing men from a rational assessment of politics."

But Machiavelli goes further. And this is where his insights directly apply in our lives, because he says that the human condition will never improve until we acknowledge our true nature. Invoking his literary hero Dante, Machiavelli suggests that "the true way to Paradise is to learn the way to Hell in order to flee from it."

However metaphorical, this advice can also be applied to our own struggles (some of which are more hellish than others) to come into our own as mothers and fathers. And by that I mean that even in the best of circumstances, parenthood is both a joy and a burden. The joy part is easy. The hard part, especially in our own politically correct times, arises from the fact that very few people are willing to admit that parenting can be and sometimes is a burden, especially for those of us not willing or able to acknowledge our own true nature. Yet, it is only by confronting our true nature that we can see what is preventing us from becoming the kind of person—and parent—that we aspire to be.

It's human nature to blame our shortcomings on external things—our busy schedules, our demanding bosses, or lack of money or moral support. But if we want to truly improve our lives—and the lives of our kids, by extension—we must acknowledge that our greatest flaws stem from within.

For me, that meant acknowledging that I can be selfish with my time, stubborn, defensive, and quick to retreat into my own little world when my kids are driving me nuts. Fortunately, I haven't seen any evidence to suggest that I have passed these negative behaviors and traits on to them. If anything, they're far more virtuous than I am, and they constantly amaze me with their kindness, compassion, and unconditional love of one another.

This hopeful state of affairs was thrown into relief one day when Teddy told me that she had submitted an essay in a writing contest at her school, the theme of which was diversity, of all things.

"Diversity? Wow," I said with surprise. "What'd you write about?"

"Katie," she said matter-of-factly.

"Can I read it?" I asked.

"Yeah," she said as she smiled. "I got second place and it's hanging in the library at school."

When she later showed me her essay, which had a picture of Katie and her above it, I smiled and felt my throat tighten as I read it. This is what she wrote:

THIS IS KATIE
Diversity in Two Sisters by Teddy Evans King.

Katie is my sister. She is very different. She has Down syndrome and her brain does not work as fast as other kids, but she is still a great sister. We love playing together and having fun playing with our cat Blackie and her kittens. We're very different, but we're still sisters.

This was better than any maxim I could read or any advice I could hope to receive. My daughter had set a much-needed example for me, one that Machiavelli would have applauded in that she had confronted reality head-on and had seen beyond Katie's disability to the true nature of things.

As Teddy was putting on her pajamas that night, I came into her room and reached into the top drawer of her dresser. "I have a surprise," I said, pulling out our beloved white, furless, stuffed kitten. (The presumed recent loss of Special Kitty had weighed heavily on both of us. It wasn't just another stuffed toy. It symbolized and celebrated Teddy's birth and the deep bond of love and affection between us. In many ways, Special Kitty symbolized "us.")

"Special Kitty!" she gasped. "Where'd you find her?"

"She was stuck between the wall and the foot of your bed."

"She was here the whole time?"

"Yep."

Teddy was quiet for a while, then asked, "Will you tell me the story again about why you named her that?"

I nodded and sat next to her on the bed. "Because it took me seven years to get pregnant with you," I said, "and when I found out that I was finally pregnant, I was so shocked and excited that I didn't know what to do, so I just grabbed my little stuffed kitten—"

"Special Kitty," she interjected.

"Yes," I said, "and jumped up and down with her in front of the mirrored closets in my bedroom."

"And then you slept with her every night until I was born," Teddy said. "And that's why all her fur is rubbed off."

"Exactly."

"I'm so glad you found her," she whispered.

"Me, too," I said softly, "and if things ever get too crazy around here and you want to stay with Dad more often, just ask, okay, because I just want you to be happy."

She got quiet again, then smiled and said, "Thanks, Mom."

And as I kissed her good night, that strange sense of peace and well-being rose up inside me again. Because even though I had just confronted my worst fear as her parent, I knew that she and I, as mother and child, were going to be just fine, regardless of how many nights she might spend away from me and with her father.

When it comes to the hard realities of life, sometimes the best thing we can do for ourselves and for our kids is to acknowledge the truth, move through it, and move forward together with our lives. Or, as Machiavelli would advise, the true way to paradise is to learn the way to hell (or whatever parental dilemma we might find ourselves in) so that we will know how to find our way out of it.

XIX

Deliverance Is of No Use Which Does Not Depend upon Yourself:
Developing Self-Reliance

Besides, there is my desire that these Medici princes should begin to engage my services, even if they should start out by having me roll along a stone. For then, if I could not win them over, I should have only myself to blame.

Machiavelli, letter to Francesco Vettori, 1513

After all the ups and downs, I was back on the right path with my kids. But in focusing so closely on my journey with them, I had ignored some deep-seated conflicts in my marriage, ones that, like the truth when buried underground (to paraphrase French philosopher Émile Zola), had been growing, choking, and gathering such an explosive force that on the day they burst out, they threatened to blow up everything with them.

If that sounds dramatic, it was, because as I neared the end of my Machiavellian experiment, Eric and I weren't just bickering but were battling over everything.

"We can fight over a piece of Swiss cheese," he once quipped about this.

And he was right. Rarely did a day or night go by that we didn't disagree on something. And like many parents of young kids—studies show that marital satisfaction drops precipitously after the first child arrives—most of our disagreements stemmed from the fact that we had major differences of opinion on many aspects of parenting. Which would have been fine had we been able to compromise or at least agree to disagree on certain things. But sometimes we couldn't, and it seemed like he was suddenly criticizing me on everything I did—or didn't do—as a parent.

When Katie would misbehave, he'd blame me for not disciplining her, when, in fact, disciplining her was all I had been doing since the day she began drawing on walls with my lipstick and dumping cold beverages on my laptop.

When Trevor wouldn't immediately say "please" or "thank you," Eric would claim I was too lax. (In fact, saying "please" and "thank you" is one of the cardinal rules that I had been consistently and insistently drilling into all of my kids since the day they realized I was doing them a huge favor by changing their diapers.)

And when my workload piled up and I needed Katie's babysitter to watch her into the evenings or asked my mom to help out with Teddy and Trevor, he'd accuse me of not wanting to spend time with my kids.

"You don't even like being with your kids," he sneered one night. "Your favorite thing to do is to sit at your computer and write."

"Stop saying that!" I snapped. "I love being with my kids and I like to write! What's wrong with that?"

"You're selfish with your time," he snarled.

"Well, you're a narcissist!" I hissed. "And you think you're always right!"

"I am always right."

"Oh really? Is it right to always criticize your wife?"

That particular spat broke out at the end of a long day, one that Eric had spent working alone in his office but that I had spent cooking, cleaning, vacuuming, sweeping, and shuttling a carload of kids around town every half hour while trying to get some work done in between.

To be fair, I could empathize with his predicament. Having spent most of his adult life traveling the world as a professional golfer, he was now married with four kids and working hard—harder, in fact, than he had ever worked in his life—to help support our family. Still . . . I didn't think it was particularly equitable or fair that he was free to leave the house every morning at seven or eight and work as late as eight or nine p.m., because I was working equally hard while running our whole household mostly alone.

You know what I'm talking about, right? And it really *isn't* fair. But this division of labor in family affairs can be traced all the way back to prehistoric days when *Homo erectus* crawled out of his cave to hunt and gather all day with his pals while his better half stayed home to care for and protect the little ones.

But that's ancient history, as they say. And anyway, one of my biggest issues with my husband didn't involve providing for our family but the more contemporary issue of "entertaining" our kids.

As a very charismatic, fun-loving guy, Eric thinks that it constitutes cruel and unusual punishment when parents force their kids to find ways to entertain themselves when they're bored. Instead, he believes the kids should spend virtually all of their free time outside—riding scooters, skateboards, tricycles, and bikes; going swimming, fishing, boating, or hiking; or otherwise frolicking all day at the beach, on a playground, or at the park.

Don't get me wrong: I agree that kids should be physically fit and have plenty of fun times outside. It's healthy. I get it. But I also firmly believe that they need an equal amount of quiet time to engage in other more creative, imaginative, introspective, and cerebral endeavors. Kids, I believe, benefit from being able to figure out how to have a good time on their own, rather than constantly being "scheduled" with nonstop activities.

One Sunday Daniel woke at dawn, beelined it to the master bedroom, and announced that he was bored. "Can I ride my skateboard?" he asked as I rubbed sleep from my eyes.

"Sure, buddy," Eric chirped, jumping out of bed like a soldier obeying a sergeant.

"Can't you wait until a little later?" I asked. "It's not fair to our neighbors to wake them up so early on a Sunday."

This naturally fell on deaf ears. And off they went. After Daniel got bored of his skateboard, they played basketball, rode bikes, tossed a football around, played catch, and then grabbed their swim trunks and jumped in the community pool.

All before nine a.m.

And when they returned to the house, Daniel plopped down on the couch, ate a few bites of cereal, and announced again that he was bored.

I say, what's wrong with allowing our kids to get bored every now and then anyway? I mean, it's not like their muscles are going to atrophy if they sit still for a few hours and quietly read, write, or just stare at the wall and think, "Jeez, I'm *so* bored!" Should it always be up to us, as parents, to entertain our kids? Don't they need to develop the muscles and initiative to do that for themselves? Maybe a little boredom now and again might be good for kids.

Boredom, of course, was something that Machiavelli battled after he lost his job and was sent to live in the Tuscan countryside with his wife and six young kids—so much so that it would prompt him to sit down and write his little primer on politics, a short and impulsive work that would ensure his place in political and literary history. In fact, it's in *The Prince* and its final chapters where Machiavelli's prose soars, as he returns to his vision of a strong, unified Italy, one brimming with renewed strength and taking her place among powerful nations. It would be another three and a half centuries before Italy was united as a nation, but he clung firmly to his dream as he "fattened and polished" his masterpiece in the winter of 1513.

In the evenings, as he put pen to paper and pondered Italy's fate, he saw man's natural slothfulness as the main obstacle keeping his homeland from achieving its glorious potential. "It is a common defect in man," he proclaims, "not to make any provision in the calm against the tempest." By this he means that some Italian princes lost their states because of their lack of bravery and military strength. They "fled when they should have defended themselves." They remained idle in peaceful times, never anticipating times of crisis. And when conquered, they kicked back and hoped that the people would recall them. They weren't bored so much as lazy, he felt. Too much Mediterranean sun, maybe.

But, as Machiavelli explicitly cautions throughout his book, it's always foolish to depend upon others for survival. Instead, he insists, a prince's best defense is his own valor. Machiavelli is speaking of the princes of Italy here, but when read closely it seems that he is speaking also of himself. Struggling to support his young family, totally bored out of his gourd, and with no hope of immediate employment, he could depend only upon only himself and his own valor.

In Latin, the word *valore* connotes courage, worthiness, and strength, and if Machiavelli was anything, he was courageous and strong and he didn't seem to fear much of anything except boredom and death. How do I know this? Because he says as much in a letter he wrote to his friend Vettori, the newly appointed Florentine ambassador to the Medici pope in Rome. It's one of the most celebrated letters in all of Italian literature, and Machiavelli sets forth in it his methods and motives in writing his masterpiece:

When evening comes, I return to my house and enter my study; on the threshold I take off my ordinary clothes, covered with mud and dirt, and wrap myself in robes meant for a court or palace. Dressed appropriately, I enter the ancient courts filled with ancient men where, affectionately received, I nourish myself on that food that alone is mine and for which I was born; where I am unashamed to converse and ask them to explain their actions, and where they, kindly, answer me. And for four hours at a time I feel no boredom, I forget all my troubles, I have no fear of poverty, or even of death . . .

Here, Machiavelli is equating boredom with death, suggesting that there exists a direct, linear descent from stasis or boredom to his own presumed early ignoble death. If this is true, then it's not too much to say that *The Prince* was born not only out of a moment of intense personal and professional crisis, but an intense existential crisis brought on by the mind-numbingly tedious and oppressively isolating tyranny of boredom. His enforced early retirement was his own private hell, one that he woke to each day and only found flight from in his late-night deliberations with ancient men.

A nice Chianti probably helped, too.

Either way, it's not surprising that he alludes in the same letter to Sisyphus, the ancient Greek mythological figure who was doomed to push a boulder up a hill, only to watch it roll back down and repeat the same boring, solitary task day after day for eternity. "Besides, there is my desire that these Medici princes should begin to engage my services," Machiavelli complains, "even if they should start out by having me roll along a stone. For then, if I could not win them over, I should have only myself to blame."

And let me ask here if there is anything more important but mind-numbingly tedious than our own daily parenting routines, especially when our children are young? We wake at dawn to feed, burp, cuddle, play, bathe, change, read, and sing and rock them back to sleep on and on ad infinitum until we collapse in exhaustion, only to wake the next day to repeat the same tasks over and over again for what seems, in our worst moments, like an eternity.

And while I don't know if Machiavelli would agree with me on this, I do believe that boredom is a critical catalyst for creativity. When we are bored, new ideas open up to us. Wasn't Newton supposedly languishing beneath an apple tree when he discovered the law of gravity? Wasn't Archimedes, the greatest mathematician of antiquity and perhaps of all time, wallowing in a bath when clarity struck? And wasn't Machiavelli bored out of his gourd when he sat down to write his masterpiece?

Boredom, then, shouldn't be feared but embraced. When it beckons us, we (and our kids) should pursue it because that's when inspiration often strikes. If you disagree, consider the words of Walt Disney, who once said that "Mickey Mouse popped out of my mind onto a drawing pad twenty years ago on a train ride from Manhattan to Hollywood at a time when business fortunes of my brother Roy and myself were at lowest ebb and disaster seemed right around the corner."

Imagine that! The idea that would lead to the Magical

Kingdom—the "Happiest Place on Earth"—and the entire Disney empire was born on a long, boring cross-country train ride.

How's that for boredom paying off?

When we are constantly stimulated or entertained, there's no space in our brains for new ideas to pop up—and that is precisely why I believe so deeply in the need for us as parents to bestow the gift of boredom on our kids.

I haven't always felt this way, of course, and as a child one of my greatest fears other than butterflies, snakes, earthquakes, and great white sharks was of being bored. I hated how excruciatingly slow time ticked by and the seemingly inescapable, suffocating sense of having nothing to do and nowhere to go. Yet, my parents rarely came to my aid when I waged yet another battle against that dreaded monster Boredom. Instead, they left me alone to stare it square in its terrible face.

One hot August day I sat like a dramatic eight-year-old zombie on the bottom step of our avocado-green-colored shag-carpeted stairs and stared at the wall until my mother rushed by with an armful of laundry, at which point I looked up at her and whined, "I'm *so* bored, I can't take it anymore!"

Instead of snuggling up next to me and suggesting something fun we could do—Disneyland! Knott's Berry

Farm! Or even the friggin' park!—she just looked at me and said very softly but sternly, "Life is boring only to the boring."

And then she disappeared behind the laundry room door.

"Hrumph," I pouted, even more bored than I was before. But as I sat there staring at the wall clarity struck. I can either keep sitting here being bored, I thought, or I can go try to find something to do. With this glimpse of the obvious, I slithered outside and filled an old tin watering can to the rim with water and spent the rest of the afternoon making mud cookies and cakes and pies.

"Still bored?" my mom called out from the porch just before dinnertime.

Covered head to toe in mud, I just shook my head and smiled.

Life is boring only to the boring.

It was a small but significant lesson, and yet, as I grew older, playing in the mud naturally lost its appeal and so, to fight off boredom, I eventually turned to books, and a whole new world opened up to me, one that magically transported me to Narnia, Oz, Never Never Land, and many other strange and amazing imaginary places.

Flash forward four decades to a cold winter day when I decided to bestow the gift of boredom on my own kids. I had just picked up Teddy from school and as I sat at my laptop, she made a quick afternoon snack. Not more than two or three minutes had passed when she looked at me and asked, "What are we gonna do now, Mom? I'm *so* bored!"

Thinking of my own mother, I turned to her and said softly but sternly, "Life is boring only to the boring."

"Huh?" she said, like I'd just spoken in some strange foreign tongue.

"Life is boring only to the boring," I repeated. "That's what Grandma always said to me when I was your age, and it means that if you can't find ways to entertain yourself, then you're probably gonna be bored. A lot."

As a strange expression spread across her face, she grabbed her snack and shuffled up to her room. After a half hour or so, she raced downstairs and dropped a little hand-written gift on my lap.

"What's this?" I asked.

"A biography of Seabiscuit," she smiled with pride.

Granted, it was taken almost verbatim from Wikipedia. Nevertheless, she had successfully waged her own battle against boredom with an amazing display of creativity and imagination.

Since that day, she has written a biography of Martin Luther King Jr. and his "I Have a Dream Speech," and is now deciding whether to write her next biography on Muppets creator Jim Hensen, Secretariat, Steve Jobs, or Cleopatra. Had I simply relented to her desperate requests for entertainment, she might not have learned how to entertain herself, a critical skill, and very valuable gift, that will hopefully last her a lifetime.

Meanwhile Daniel, as he grew older, was growing increasingly independent and physically absent from our daily life. Like many young boys, he loves sports and is currently playing team baseball, soccer, and football and just began Junior Lifeguards—which collectively claim most of his spare time. But even though I happen to think that allowing a child to compete in so many sports seems a bit overwhelming (it certainly would be for me!), for Daniel it's heaven. He absolutely loves it—the competition, the clamor, the group dynamic, and the athleticism, which is great—and what can I say; he's his father's son. At the end of the day, I guess some kids are conditioned or just naturally inclined for more quiet contemplation. Others are always rarin' to go go go. And that's okay.

Still, I do believe that too many parents these days are afraid to bestow the gift of boredom on their kids. Instead, they fill their days with endless, frenetic, often meaningless activity. In structuring their days this way we are, it seems, creating a generation of activity addicts, which is not only a great disservice to our kids but, if we agree that without boredom we might not have *The Prince* and many other great works of literature, art, poetry, philosophy, and science, is also a grave disservice to modern society.

One way, perhaps the only way, out of this trap is to simply allow our kids to be bored. If we can do this, then once again the ends (amazing displays of creativity and imagination) will justify the means (refusing to constantly entertain them).

The task that remained for me was to convince my husband of this.

That, of course, would be easier said than done, as this particular issue both reflected and embraced a huge difference between Eric and me. I'm naturally introspective and quiet, preferring a good book to a raucous party. He's outgoing, the life of the party, and always eager to say yes to every invitation and meet the next friend. And, yet, while we are both independent, very different, and tend to battle it out to the bitter end a lot, we do have great love and respect for each other—and one thing's for certain. I'm *never* bored!

But, because this book is called *Machiavelli for Moms* and not *Machiavelli for Marriage*, I'll simply add that yet another one of Machiavelli's maxims spoke to me. That maxim: "In all Cities and all Peoples there Exists and Has Always Existed the Same Desires and Passions." With this in mind, and by objectively (as opposed to idealistically) assessing the state of my marriage, as Machiavelli would advise, I was able to see that even though my husband and I have had some major differences of opinion over the years, when it comes to our children, our family, and our marriage, there exists and has always existed the same desires and passions.

And that maxim contains an important kernel of truth for all people in all places, whether you're a Renaissance prince trying to maintain a well-ordered state or a modern-day mom or dad trying to raise a happy, well-mannered family. If your passions and desires—your ultimate ends—are always the same, that's all that really matters at the end of the day.

Bottom line: like motherhood, marriage is hard, and exponentially more so when you add kids to the mix. You don't need Machiavelli to tell you that. But here's what I learned from him about being married with kids: accept conflict as a given, choose your battles wisely, and focus on what unites you and your spouse instead of what divides you and drives you batty.

And when you're in the wrong, or even when you're not, try this little disarming trick: stare your spouse square in the eye, then smile sweetly and say, "I'm sorry. I was a jackass." If you can do that, your battle will stop dead in its tracks and you and your better half will have a much-needed laugh. In other words, when it comes to marriage and parenting, a sense of common purpose and unity combined with a sense of humor is sometimes, if not always, the best strategy. And I'm convinced, for reasons you'll see, that Machiavelli would agree with me on this.

XX

On Humor:
Machiavelli's Lighter Side

> We now know that [Machiavelli] responded with that smile to the
> miseries of life, to keep from being overwhelmed by grief, outrage,
> and melancholy and to keep from giving men and Fortune the cruel
> satisfaction of seeing him weep. Still, the smile was more than just a
> defense against life; it was also his way of immersing himself in life.
>
> Maurizio Viroli, *Niccolò's Smile*

So, we all know that "Machiavellian" is a byword
for treachery, mendacity, and the cunning and ruthless use of power. But what I learned as I neared
the end of *The Prince* is that Machiavelli was a very warm,
witty guy who, while tactless at times, was well loved by
his friends for his bawdy, ironic, self-deprecating sense of
humor. And if he was "refreshingly free from conventional
thinking in his published writing," as one observer put it,
"he was even more iconoclastic, funny, self-deprecating and
ironic in his private conversation and correspondence."

How so?

Well, when he learned at the time of his father's burial

that other folks had been surreptitiously using the family tomb, he didn't get angry or try to get even. Instead, he simply replied, "Let them be, for my father was a great lover of conversation, and the more there are to keep him company, the more pleased he will be."

That's kind of witty, right? Or is it just me?

Either way, there's a lot of evidence in Machiavelli's letters and in those of his contemporaries that suggests that he was a very likable, down-to-earth guy who was probably a blast to hang out with in local taverns and bars. But it was his poems, tales, and plays that gave me the clearest glimpse of his lascivious imagination and wit. In his comedic play *Clizia*, for example, he mocks the folly of an older man's pursuit of a beautiful younger woman, and in the novella *Belfagor* his protagonist must choose between the torments of hell and the anxiety of marriage. Ha! I thought. Anyone who's been married with kids for long enough can see the humor in that, right?

Even the dark and brooding German philosopher Friedrich Nietzsche found humor in Machiavelli's prose, noting that in *The Prince* he "lets us breathe the dry, refined air of Florence and cannot help presenting the most serious matters in a boisterous *allegrissimo*, perhaps not without a malicious artistic sense of the contrast he risks—long, difficult, hard, dangerous thoughts and . . . the very best, most capricious humor."

As I thought about this, I realized that I'd seen evidence of Machiavelli's "capricious humor" and "malicious artistic sense" all along. It was right there, in his maxim that a prince must not dispossess the people of their possessions because "men sooner forget the death of their father than the loss of their inheritance." But Machiavelli's not condoning or encouraging such behavior. He's simply saying, with his wicked, deadpan wit, that men can and sometimes do behave this way. Dark, yes—but an example no less of how his stark aphorisms and advice might "bring a smile to the lips" of anyone willing to ask hard questions about the dark reality of human nature.

But I came across the most startling example of his lascivious wit in a 1509 letter he wrote to his friend Luigi Guicciardini. In it, he tells a story about an encounter he supposedly had with a grotesque old hag whom he was tricked into having sex with one day in Lombardy. To paraphrase it couldn't possibly do it justice. But I will because it's a hilariously ridiculous read (although I don't think Marietta would agree).

"Damn it all, Luigi!" he begins. "You see how fortune can bring about in men different results in similar matters. You, when you have screwed her once, you still get the urge to screw her again." He then recounts his own recent foray in a dimly lit room, only to discover, after the fact, that he had been sorely duped.

"My God!" he writes. "The woman was so ugly that I almost dropped dead." On the top of her bald head, he said, "were a number of lice taking a stroll"; her "eyebrows were full of nits"; "one eye looked up and the other down"; her "nostrils were full of snot and one of them was cut off"; and "her mouth looked like Lorenzo de' Medici's" but "it was twisted on one side and drooled a bit since she had no teeth to keep the saliva in her mouth. And I swear to God!"

he wickedly quips, "I don't believe my lust will return as long as I am in Lombardy."

Did this actually happen? Who knows. But that's not the point. What matters is that Machiavelli was a master at finding humor in the ridiculous. And his humor, I learned, wasn't lost on his confidants. "When your amusing, witty and pleasant conversation echoes about our ears," one friend writes, "it relieves, cheers and refreshes us."

Okay, so Machiavelli was a witty, well-liked guy. So what? Why do we care? And what does it have to do with our own ridiculously busy lives as modern-day mothers and fathers?

Quite a bit, I would submit, because we can all learn a thing or two from his capacity to laugh at himself in even the grimmest of situations. Nowhere does this come out more clearly than in a letter he wrote after being tortured on the strappado in a "dank, vermin-infested" prison after being unjustly arrested for his alleged role in a failed conspiracy to assassinate Cardinal Giuliano de' Medici and seize the government by force.

"I have on my legs a set of fetters," he writes, "with six pulls of the cord on my shoulders; my other miseries I do not intend to recount . . . since so the poets are treated! These broken walls generate lice so swollen," he adds, "that they look like flies; never was there such a stench . . . as in my so dainty hospice."

Instead of wallowing in self-pity, Machiavelli responds to this reversal of fortune with "a wisecrack and a shrug." "The image of his 'dainty hospice' crawling with lice who fatten themselves on the wasting flesh of prisoners is half farce, half tragedy," biographer Miles Unger writes, "a play of light and shadow that runs through both his political and literary works."

Light and shadow. We can all relate to that in our own lives, right?

But Machiavelli didn't just find humor in this grim situation. He chose to view it as "something of a character-building exercise." A few weeks after his release, while still recuperating from his injuries, he wrote to Vettori: "And as for turning my face toward fortune, you should take at least this pleasure from these troubles of mine, that I bore them with such stoicism that I am proud and esteem myself more highly than before."

And that, I thought, is yet another great example for all modern moms, which is this: we would all be well advised to try to maintain a sense of humor in times of adversity and crisis. Machiavelli was a master at this, as is reflected in a letter he wrote near the end of his life in which he cites lines from one of Petrarch's sonnets: "if at times I laugh or sing / I do so because I have no other way than this / To give vent to my bitter tears."

Poor guy.

But here's the bottom line: there's a thin line that separates laughter and pain, comedy and tragedy, humor and hurt, as humorist Erma Bombeck observed. And that, I would add, is another fate we can't ever escape. So what do we do?

Laugh and sing, my friend. Laugh and friggin' sing— just like Machiavelli.

XXI

One Who Relies Entirely on Fortune Is Lost:
Taking Matters into Your Own Hands

Machiavelli horrifies and repels us, yet also attracts and fascinates.

Hanna Pitkin, *Fortune Is a Woman*

ore than a year had passed since I had made my first Machiavellian move. And despite a few disasters and some agonizing defeats, all was now (mostly) peaceful and serene on the home front. Teddy and Daniel were still happy, well behaved, and doing fantastic in school. Katie was thriving in her new special-ed class and had been granted a part-time, one-on-one aide. And Trevor was making lots of friends at preschool. So, late one night, I turned to the final pages of *The Prince* and came across Machiavelli's most detailed, if shocking, discussion of Fortuna, the goddess of fortune and personification of good or bad luck.

As with "virtù," Machiavelli's use of the term "Fortuna" is often confusing. But at the most basic level he's referring to man's fortune in the face of the capricious malice of fate. While most classical representations of Fortuna portrayed her as a "mostly benign if fickle goddess" and a "font of human goods as well as evils," Machiavelli depicts her as a "malevolent and uncompromising source of human misery, affliction, and disaster."

Just what we need.

But while Machiavelli cautions that no one can act effectively when directly opposed by Fortuna, he concedes that we are not totally defenseless against her fury. He clarifies this with an analogy. Invoking the brutal forces of nature, he says first that Fortuna resembles "one of our destructive rivers which, when it is angry, turns the plains into lakes, throws down the trees and buildings, takes earth from one spot, puts it in another; everyone flees before the flood; everyone yields to its fury and no one can repel it."

Sounds bad, I know. But he leaves us with a glimmer of hope by saying that man can defend himself against Fortuna. For "when the weather becomes fair" he can erect barriers and defenses "in such a manner that, rising again, the waters may pass away by canal and their force be neither so unrestrained nor so dangerous." We can resist her fury, Machiavelli concludes, but only if through wisdom, foresight, and virtù we are prepared for her inevitable arrival. In other words, if the skies are blue and seas are smooth right now, don't kick back and pamper yourself with a leisurely mani-pedi. Instead, stay on your toes so that when disaster strikes—and it will—you're ready to take any means necessary to survive.

Building on this, Machiavelli cites the desperate plight of Italy in the early sixteenth century. Relatively peaceful, powerful, and prosperous only a few decades earlier, the region was now being torn apart by warring factions and at risk of being conquered by the powerful, rapacious foreign nations of Germany, France, and Spain, as well as the Holy Roman Empire.

"Without barriers and without any defense," Italy, Machiavelli says, "was invaded and conquered by barbarians." But had it been "defended by proper valor either this invasion wouldn't have made the great changes it has made or it would not have come about at all." For too long, the princes of Italy had depended on good fortune to keep the enemies at bay. But this, Machiavelli laments, was not unforeseeable, for a prince who "relies entirely on fortune is lost" while "he who suits his conduct to the spirit of the times will be successful."

If it seems like he's repeating himself, he is, until he delivers his most shocking analogy of all. "It is better to be adventurous than cautious because fortune is a woman," he proclaims, "and if you wish to keep her under it is necessary to beat her," as it has been seen that "she allows herself to be mastered by the adventurous rather than by those who go to work more coldly." Fortune, therefore, he concludes, "is always woman-like, a lover of young men because they are less cautious, more dominant, and with more audacity, command her."

Yikes is right! But maybe he forgot to take out the trash and had a little spat with his wife right before he wrote that.

Either way, here's the takeaway: fortune demands an aggressive response, or she will destroy those of us who are too cautious or cowardly to dominate her. And that is what

virtù, the touchstone of princely and parental success, pro-
vides: the courage, wisdom, foresight, flexibility, ingenuity,
insight, and ability to respond to the contingencies of life
by any means necessary to survive.

As fortune would have it, I, like Machiavelli, found myself
suddenly unemployed in my mid-forties, just as I was nearing the end of my experiment. But, armed with his advice,
I didn't freak out, at least not immediately. What I quickly
learned, however, is that being a mother in her mid-forties
with four young kids doesn't exactly make one a highly, or
even slightly, competitive candidate.

This state of affairs began inauspiciously enough. It was
a Tuesday afternoon. Teddy was reading. I was writing a
brief. Trevor and Katie were playing with Hot Wheels and
blocks on the floor. And my cell phone rang.

"Who is it? Dad?" Teddy asked as I glanced at the number flashing on the screen.

"No," I sighed. "It's my boss."

"Are you gonna answer it?" she asked.

It was a nice quiet moment with my kids, one that
I cherished, so I hesitated and let it go to voice mail. "I'll
call him back," I said guiltily.

A few minutes later, I did just that. His voice was flat as
he asked me to come into the office the next day to drop off
some legal files.

"Sure, no problem," I said agreeably. "What time?"

"Noon," he said, then thanked me and hung up.

When I arrived at his office the next day, his assistant greeted me without smiling and stood up. "I'll tell him you're here," she said, then disappeared.

Moments later, my boss entered the room, closed the door, and leaned tensely against a cabinet. The expression on his thin, Ichabod Crane–like face was serious, and faint beads of sweat glistened on his forehead.

Still, I was oblivious to the news that was coming my way.

"Suzy, the quality of your briefs has been declining, and we need to be able to get ahold of you at all times between nine and five," he said. "So, I'm going to have to let you go."

Stunned, I stared him square in his eye. "You're firing me?" I said incredulously.

"It's a business decision," he said, fidgeting with his tie.

I couldn't believe it. He had always gone out of his way to effusively praise my briefs and I had worked diligently for him for two years. (Well, one year and 363 days, to be exact, which had significant implications for my annual vacation days allotment, which would have vested in two days—a legitimate if ruthless Machiavellian move on his part, right?)

"You always tell me how excellent my briefs are and how valuable I am to your office," I reminded him. "And I have your voice mails to prove it."

"Again, it's a business decision" was all that he offered.

While it was true that I wasn't always available during the day when he called, now I was fuming. "I've worked

my ass off for you for two years and have the highest winning appeal ratio of anyone here."

He grunted his denial and placed a crumpled check on
the desk. "This is your full unused vacation time," he said,
then headed for the door.

"I'm calling a lawyer!" I threatened. "And I hope for
your sake you didn't replace me with someone younger
than forty-one," I added in a lawyerly way, knowing that
that's the age at which federal anti–age discrimination stat-
utes kick in (and not yet knowing that my replacement was
in fact older than that).

But to no avail.

Just as Machiavelli was unceremoniously dismissed
from his position after many years of faithful service, I,
too, had suffered the same fate. And just as Machiavelli
diligently searched for a new gig right away to support
his family, I dutifully did the same. But my most recent
job searches had been in my late thirties and early forties,
which is one thing. Looking for employment as a forty-
five-year-old mother of four is an entirely different matter.
Here's an example of how things generally went down:

I find my old navy blue business suit in the back of my
closet behind some pregnancy clothes. I squeeze into it.
I greet the babysitter. Then I enter an impeccably appointed
law office and sit at a conference table across from three
middle-aged senior partners. Out the window behind them
I see dark clouds gathering over the Pacific Ocean.

"You certainly have an impressive résumé, Suzanne,"
says one of them. "Law Review. A PhD from Berkeley.
And experience as an appellate brief writer."

"What we need," says another, "is a strong writer, and, well, it looks like you're a perfect fit for us."

All the partners nod.

"We'd need you to begin immediately," says the female partner. "Within the next week or two, and the salary would be within your requested range. And you would be able to work primarily from your home."

"That sounds great," I smile, proud of myself.

"And you wrote a book on the Holocaust?" the first one says. "I'm kind of a history buff."

Prepared, I hand my book to him and he eagerly flips through it. "When did you find the time to write this?" he asks.

I wistfully laugh. "Before I had kids."

Dead silence.

"I see," the female partner replies, her voice suddenly tight with concern. "And how many kids do you have?"

Not seeing the problem, I playfully make the shape of a gun with my fingers, point it at my temple, then pull the trigger and say, "Four."

More silence; then: "In high school? College?"

Now I see the problem. "Uh, no," I backtrack, trying to diminish the damage. "They're nine, eight, five, and three. But . . . they're *very* independent . . . and I have a really reliable babysitter . . . Really . . . reliable . . ."

The partners shoot looks at one another.

"Well, thank you for coming in today," they say. "We have several more applicants to interview, but we'll be back in touch real soon."

"How soon?" I ask, standing up.

"A month or two."

Yeah, right.

For women but not typically for men, having young kids presents a severe impediment, if not a tightly closed door, to career advancement. So, sadly, does being in your mid-forties. Here's how that dirty little secret among some youth-oriented employers goes down:

I'm seated in a reception room with three female job candidates, all in their late twenties. A door swings open and a stunning female lawyer in her early thirties strides out, followed by a beautiful blond legal secretary in her late twenties.

"Right this way, ma'am," she says, smiling falsely at me.

I follow her into a conference room, where two nattily dressed male partners in their mid-thirties review my résumé from which I have strategically deleted all references to graduation dates that would reveal my "advanced" age.

"You have an amazing résumé," one partner says. "But, to be honest, we're looking for someone right out of law school."

"You mean someone younger than forty-one?" I ask.

"Well, yes," the other one mumbles.

"It's not even legal to say that," I remind them.

"Say what?" they shrug, feigning innocence.

But instead of getting all up in arms about it, I chose to use this situation to my advantage by turning it into an opportunity to forge a new career path. I didn't want to be a disability brief writer (too disillusioning and depressing) or divorce lawyer (ditto, times ten) anymore anyway.

Don't get me wrong: I have always been grateful to

have had the opportunity to go to law school, and while I do love the study of law, I didn't particularly enjoy practicing it. My first "true love"—professionally and intellectually—has, as I mentioned, always been history. And from a very young age I had always loved to write. Could I combine the two? Should I finally try to rely not on an employer but on myself to continue contributing my half of what it takes to support my family? Big decisions. And big stakes. Still, I'd always been a firm believer in that old adage that the greatest regret we will have at the end of our lives is not what we did but what we didn't do—or at least try to do. And so, after much thought, I decided that I would try to earn a living as a writer, something that I had long dreamed of doing and that, if it panned out, would allow me to stay at home with my kids, at least until they were safely away at college or otherwise living independently as young adults. And in this major midlife career move, I was taking my cue from Machiavelli.

In what ways?

Well, when he finally realized that his little masterpiece didn't impress or even catch the attention of the Medicis and wasn't going to result in a new job, he slowly came to peace with it and committed himself to a life as a writer. Even before he finished *The Prince*, he returned to his *Discourses on Livy*, a much longer and more thoughtful book, then turned his restless mind to other political works, as well as many poems, tales, and plays, one of which—*The Mandragola*—was performed widely during his lifetime and is still considered by many today to be one of Italy's greatest plays.

As fortune would have it, his prodigious literary output eventually put him in the good graces of the powers that be and, in 1520, he received an official commission from Cardinal Giulio de' Medici to write a history of Florence as he saw fit.

Machiavelli's virtù and perseverance had at last paid off.

The wheel of fortune had finally—if only temporarily—turned his way.

And with this example in mind, I carefully placed my old copy of *The Prince* back up on the shelf and began writing, hoping that my own virtù and perseverance might one day pay a few dividends, too. And if it did, I thought as I pondered the future, the best part of all would be that I would have the freedom to work at home all day while caring for my kids in my tattered old expandable-waist, post-pregnancy sweatpants.

What more could a mom want than that?

And if it seems like we're right back where we started, we are—and we aren't. Yeah, I'm still in my sweatpants. But my kids are happier, my marriage is stronger and saner, and I've found a career that I really love. We're the same big, boisterous family we've always been—but many essential things have changed. "What is essential," Antoine de Saint-Exupéry writes in *The Little Prince*, "is invisible to the eye."

And what I ultimately learned from my experiment with *The Prince* is this: life is hard for all moms. It always has been and will always be. So stop wallowing in self-pity like I was. Turn directly toward your most pressing problems and deal with them. You'll feel better. Then buck up, use Machiavelli's rules to take back your own kingdom, and get on with it!

Most important, be grateful for the time that you have with your kids and enjoy it—even when they're bickering, whining, shrieking, fighting, or otherwise trying to kill each other, as all kids occasionally do. If you can do that, you *will* stop daydreaming about vacationing alone in Mexico, get your healthy glow back, and begin to feel powerful, confident, proactive, competent, thankful, playful, and even frisky again. And for that you and your happy, well-mannered family will have Machiavelli to thank.

Seriously, I wouldn't kid you about something as miraculous as that.

I promise.

CONCLUSION

"The Question of Machiavelli":
Or, Machiavelli's Legacy to Us as
Modern-Day Mothers and Fathers

So, I had finished *The Prince* and my experiment had come to an end. Still, I couldn't get Machiavelli out of my mind. Something about him not only fascinated me but also haunted me, and I found myself wanting to know what others have thought about him as a man. So I did a little research and came across an intriguing essay entitled "The Question of Machiavelli" in the *New York Review of Books*. In it, historian Isaiah Berlin sets out to answer the question: "What is it that so deeply shocked so many readers of Machiavelli, who did not react similarly to equally tough-minded sentiments in Thucydides or Aristotle or the Old Testament and later writings?"

In answering that question, Berlin surveys nearly four centuries of scholarship on Machiavelli and suggests that there is "something surprising about the sheer number of interpretations of [his] political opinions" and a "startling degree of divergence about the central view, the basic political attitude of Machiavelli."

Some scholars, Berlin tells us, see Machiavelli not as the ruthless and cynical defender of fraud and deceit in statecraft but as an "anguished humanist," one who "laments the vices of men which make such wicked courses politically unavoidable." Others think he is an enlightened moralist, the man who divorced politics from ethics yet "wrings his hands over a world in which political ends can only be achieved by means that are morally evil." For others, he is a man of deep insight "into the real historical forces . . . that mold men and transform their morality," and who "rejected Christian principles for those of reason, political unity, and centralization."

Still others think Machiavelli was a supremely passionate and pragmatic patriot who saw with open eyes how Cesare Borgia, if he had lived, "might have liberated Italy from the barbarous French and Spaniards and Austrians" who had "reduced her to misery and poverty, decadence and chaos." And others still yet, as we have seen, believe that the author of *The Prince* was a satirist, for he surely could not have literally meant what he wrote. But the commonest view of Machiavelli, says Berlin, "is still that of most Elizabethans, dramatists and scholars alike, for whom he is a man inspired by the Devil to lead good men to their doom, the great subverter, the teacher of evil," the "inspirer of St. Bartholomew's Eve, the original of Iago . . . the 'murderous Machiavel' of the famous 400 references in Elizabethan literature."

So what do these competing interpretations—these many masks of Machiavelli—have to do with our lives as modern-day mothers and fathers? Quite a bit. For if you consider the startling degree of divergence in the many responsibilities and demands that press in relentlessly upon us each day as parents, you'll see that we, too, are required to wear many masks as parents. And if our children were to speculate about our own parental character and convictions, they, too, like those who have tried to peer into the mind of Machiavelli, might offer many conflicting interpretations. In observing us, they might scratch their heads and think, Jeez, sometimes Mom's totally happy, relaxed, playful, and laid-back; and sometimes she's totally frazzled, stressed-out, aggravated, and impatient. And that's okay.

Still, the sheer diversity of maxims in this experiment did make me occasionally wonder if its central premise— that almost all affairs of parenting can be viewed through a Machiavellian lens—had amounted to an inconsistent if not wholly unadvisable parental approach on my part (e.g., strictness in relation to rules and discipline; leniency in relation to sleeping arrangements; tough-mindedness in relation to manners, morality, and homework; and passionate pragmatism in relation to the preservation of order and stability in my home).

Yet, just as Machiavelli's political opinions were formulated as a means to achieve his most burning desire—that of a strong, unified, morally regenerated, and victorious Italy, whether it be saved by force, virtù, fortune, or fraud—so, too, do the many duties and responsibilities of parenting require me to adopt divergent attitudes and postures toward my children: sometimes I'm tough, sometimes lenient; sometimes I'm an idealist, sometimes a realist. But through it all, I am always loving, and just as Machiavelli's greatest desire was for the glory of his beloved Florence, my greatest desire is and will always be for the unity and stability of my family and the happiness and well-being of my kids.

But what is it about Machiavelli that has deeply shocked so many readers for nearly five centuries? Although Berlin's argument is too complex to fully address here, his conclusion is surprisingly straightforward—and important. Machiavelli's "cardinal achievement," Berlin maintains, is his "uncovering of an insoluble dilemma," one that stems from the recognition that equally legitimate ends, equally legitimate value systems may contradict or come into collision with each other without the possibility of reconciliation, and not merely in rare or exceptional circumstances, but as a normal part of the human condition.

If this is true, it undermines one central assumption of Western thought: namely, that there is one true, one final and singular solution to the question of how men should live. And therein lies Machiavelli's importance and legacy to us as modern-day parents. For if there is no one ideal way that humans should live, then it also true, by extension, that there is no one ideal way, no one ultimate set of rules by which we should raise our kids. What works for one family might lead to disaster for another—one need only watch one episode of *Celebrity Wife Swap* to confirm this—and what might seem rational to some (e.g., removing a bedroom door from its hinges and storing it in the garage) might seem downright silly or ridiculous to others.

Aside from keeping our children healthy, happy, and safe, the day-to-day decisions that we make on their behalf should be formed and informed not by what some popular professionals or parenting books say but by our *own* value systems, our *own* equally legitimate parental ends. I only share my Machiavellian approach here because it was enlightening for me, and it may or may not be enlightening for you. But if you do decide to try it, remember what I advised at the outset: don't be afraid of your power as a parent. Embrace it—then use it wisely, consistently, lovingly, and with the knowledge that when it comes to raising your own little prince or princess, sometimes the ends really *do* justify the means.

I submitted the manuscript of this book to my editor on November 1, 2012, almost exactly five hundred years to the day that Machiavelli lost his job and his entire life began to unravel. And just as he wrote *The Prince* to share with his contemporaries what he had learned about politics, I wrote this book to share with my own peers what I learned from him about parenting.

The first ten chapters or so flowed out of me, and I wrote them in roughly three months. Then I hit a roadblock—well, not so much of a roadblock as a fork in the road—and I had some decisions to make. What should I share? What should I keep private? And after much thought, I ultimately decided to share both the ups and the downs of this experiment for three main reasons, all of which are related in one way or another to what I learned from Machiavelli.

First: Machiavelli wasn't afraid to tell it like it is—and he wasn't shy about exposing his own flaws. In a similar way, I've never been overly afraid to call a spade a spade, even if that "spade" might happen to be me. So why not show my hand and let the cards fall where they may? Things get dark quick, I admit. But welcome to the brutal realism of Machiavelli! And if my approach provokes angry criticism, well, then, perhaps out of that I will either believe even more deeply in my parental convictions or further learn the errors of my ways. Either way, something will be learned—and knowledge, as Machiavelli would say, is power.

Second: Machiavelli tells us that we often learn our most valuable lessons from our own failures and mistakes, as well as from the failures and mistakes of others. Think JFK and the Bay of Pigs invasion of Cuba in 1961. What Kennedy learned about leadership from that fiasco helped him avert a far graver disaster during the Cuban Missile Crisis the following year. That said, if even only a few readers can take something away from my own victories and defeats as a mother, then this book will have served its purpose.

Third: what I admire most about Machiavelli, aside from his being a loving father, is his tough-mindedness and honesty, traits that can be successfully applied, as I have tried to show here, to both politics and parenting. These qualities carry over to Machiavelli's own authorial intent in *The Prince* when he writes, "It being my intention to write a thing which shall be useful to him who apprehends it, it appears to me more appropriate to follow up the real truth of the matter than the imagination of it." And so for these reasons "the real truth of the matter" is what I share with you here.

But what do my kids think about this book, one in which they each play a central role? Well, they haven't shown any interest in reading it yet, so that remains to be seen—although Teddy did recently draw a cover for it that has a picture of a crown followed by an equal sign followed by a big red heart in a box. What does this mean? Does it mean that she thinks Machiavelli equals love, of all things?

I don't know because I haven't asked. But that's the theory I'm sticking with because just as *The Prince* is Machiavelli's love story for his beloved Florence, this little book is my own love story for my kids, and if they do choose to read it someday, I hope they will see that nothing makes me happier or prouder than being their mom, even when they're driving me to the brink of insanity, which they still have the uncanny ability to do.

And if your kids still sometimes drive you nuts, too, then do what I do: sit back, relax, and channel Machiavelli's maxim that "the more sand that passes through the hourglass of life the more clearly we see through it." In other words, your kids are only young once, so savor this precious time that you have with them and be confident in the bittersweet knowledge that this, too, like the sand in the hourglass of life, shall soon pass. Then buck up, forge on, and remember that "he who wishes to be obeyed must know how to command."

Go get 'em! And good luck!

APPENDIX I

Take the Quiz:

Are You a Machiavellian Mom?

Give yourself one point for each statement you agree with.

Sound rules and strict discipline positively shape a child's behavior.

A child appreciates clear boundaries.

Honesty is the best policy when it comes to the big things in life.

Sometimes it's okay to tell little white lies to a child.

Children obey rules because of their fear of being punished by their parent.

If you are liberal with expenditures, you run the risk of financial ruin.

A child should study the actions of great men to learn from their example.

Letting problems develop until they're obvious to everyone is bad leadership.

If a child's every whim is indulged, s/he will tend to become ungrateful.

A blended family is more difficult to govern than a non-blended one.

Praising good behavior positively reinforces it.

Criticizing a child creates resentment and shame.

One change in family patterns leads the way to others.

If given too many material items, a child will expect more.

It is more perilous to discipline a stepchild than a biological child.

When a family problem develops, parents should act swiftly and decisively.

Humor helps people get through times of adversity and crisis.

Power is difficult to maintain without the authority to enforce it.

Lengthy, immediate time-outs are more effective than brief, non-timely ones.

For parental success, power must not only be acquired but maintained.

What works for some parents doesn't always work for others.

Flexibility helps pave the way to parental happiness and success.

If you scored between 10 and 22, you might be a Machia-vellian Mom.

If you scored between 5 and 9, you've got some work to do.

And if you scored between 0 and 4, you need to tap into your inner Prince.

APPENDIX II

Machiavelli for Kids:

The Problem

So, your mom's been reading this book and now she's acting kind of strange. Not in a bad way. Just ... different. Like, she doesn't let you jump on your bed anymore, toss dirty socks in your drawers, or throw fistfuls of cereal on the floor.

And it's making you kind of nervous, right?

But don't worry. Because if you read this, I'll tell you what she's been reading, and that will make you feel more relaxed.

And there's more.

As she begins to feel and act more powerful and confident, you will, too, because you'll know what she's secretly planning to do with you. And once you know that, you can hatch your own secret plan as a counterattack.

Sounds fun, huh?

But before we get to that, let me first tell you a bit about this Machiavelli guy. It's a weird name, I know. And if you said it out loud, it would sound something like Mack-e-uh-vel-ee.

Anyway, his first name was Niccolò. But let's just call him Nick.

So, Nick lived five hundred years ago in Florence, Italy, which is in Europe. One day, a big family of princes rode into town, kicked the old ruler out, and took power. Not long after that, Nick got fired from his job, then got tossed into prison for something he didn't do. And when he got out, things only got worse for poor Nick.

Why?

Because he had a wife and six little kids but he didn't have much money to buy food and clothes for them. He felt really bad about that, as you can imagine. So one night he decided to write a little book called *The Prince* to show those new rulers how smart he was.

Why did he do this? Because he thought it might make them like him and convince them to give him a new job.

But that didn't happen. And that's not what matters anyway.

What matters is that Nick meant *The Prince* to be a kind of "how-to" book to show the new princes of Italy how to rule over their states and make their people better behaved.

And that's where your mom comes in again, because—guess what?

She's using Nick's rules to help her rule over *your* house and make *you* better behaved! Really. I wouldn't kid you about something as serious as this.

But here's the good news. Now that you know what your mom is secretly plotting to do, you can begin secretly plotting, too.

Sound like a plan?

Okay, great. There's no time to waste. So I'll give you three quick tips to help you win this game!

1

IT'S ALL ABOUT POWER

First: whatever you do, do *not* let your mom know that you know what she knows.

Stay cool.

Remain focused.

Play dumb if you must.

And when she asks you to do something, just do it. And do it without acting all grumpy like a baby monkey about it. Because that's just embarrassing. Trust me.

And besides, if you don't do what she asks, you're

gonna lose that battle anyway. Why? Because (a) she's bigger than you, (b) she's probably stronger than you, and (c) she's prepared to give you a long time-out—and that's the last thing you want.

Right?

So, remember: it's all about power. You've got it (because *she's* asking *you* to do something). But if she thinks she does, you're golden. That's what we're going for here.

2

DON'T MISBEHAVE OR YOU'LL GET PUNISHED

Repeat after me: don't misbehave or you'll get punished. How do I know this? Because one of the first rules your mom learned from Nick is that "good laws follow from good arms."

What does this mean?

It means that she's prepared to enforce her own rules with her arms.

Sad but true, my friend. Sad but true. And if you wrote this rule as an equation in your math class, it would look like this:

YOU MISBEHAVE + YOUR MOM GETS MAD = YOU GET PUNISHED

And that's not fun for anyone.

So remember: if you always behave, you won't ever get punished. And everyone will be as happy as a rat in a cheese factory about that.

I promise.

3

FOLLOW THE RULES AND YOU'LL BE COOL

If this hasn't happened yet, it will soon: your mom will march into your room, then smile and say, "Okay, we're holding our first Family Meeting tonight to make some new family rules."

But don't panic.

You can take control of this situation and turn it to your advantage.

How? It's simple. After she lays down her rules, she's gonna let you suggest some rules of your own.

And that's when you take action.

First, if you have a brother or sister, this is what you must do: suggest some rules that you know they will break but not you. Like, if your sister whines a lot or if your brother picks his nose, then calmly raise your hand and say, "No whining! And no picking your nose!"

That's key. Because they'll be the ones who get punished and you can just kick back, relax, and laugh.

And if you don't have brothers or sisters, then do this: make some rules that you know your mom will break. That way, *she's* the one who gets punished by *you*!

See, I told you this could be fun!

But here's the catch: you've got to follow her rules, too. But that's pretty easy to do, right?

So remember: Do what your mom asks you to do. Don't misbehave. And just follow her rules and you'll be cool.

Get it? Got it? Good!

And good luck!

APPENDIX III

Machiavelli Macaroni and Cheese
(by Way of Thomas Jefferson)

So we all know that Thomas Jefferson is one of our most famous Founding Fathers. And while I don't know what Machiavelli would have made of him, I have a hunch that he would've been quite impressed with Jefferson and his many virtùs that helped him accomplish such an astonishingly wide range of things as a leader.

As a scholar, author, architect, scientist, and statesman, Jefferson applied his brilliant mind to many activities. He was elected to the Virginia House of Burgesses when he was twenty-five, served in the Continental Congress, was governor of Virginia, and was a diplomat in France, where he helped negotiate the treaties that ended the Revolutionary War.

He also founded the University of Virginia; was fluent in six languages, including Latin, French, Spanish, Italian, and Greek; and wrote the Declaration of Independence at the age of thirty-three! He then served as secretary of state under George Washington, vice president under John Adams, and, along with his good pal James Madison, wrote the Virginia and Kentucky Resolutions in defense of states' rights and the freedom of speech.

During his presidency, Jefferson did many more important things: he repealed the Alien and Sedition Acts, eliminated an unpopular whiskey tax, and sent our navy to fight Barbary pirates who were harassing American ships on the Mediterranean Sea. He also doubled the size of the country by purchasing the Louisiana Territory from Napoléon in 1803 and then commissioned Lewis and Clark to explore western lands that, back then, to most white men, were totally unknown. It's no wonder then that at a Nobel Prize dinner held at the White House in 1962, President Kennedy quipped that "so many brilliant minds have never been gathered together at the White House with the possible exception of when Thomas Jefferson dined alone."

So what *did* Jefferson eat when he dined alone?

Well, it's well known that he enjoyed fancy French cuisine, but he was also fond of fresh vegetables like English peas, tomatoes, and collard greens. He also liked homemade macaroni and cheese—and, given his many accomplishments as a virtuous leader, maybe we should call it homemade "Machiavelli Macaroni and Cheese"!

Either way, it has been said that Jefferson first served macaroni and cheese at the White House in 1802. Of course, the dish he ate is nothing like the boxed version we're familiar with today. Using pasta and Parmesan cheese imported from Italy, Jefferson's chefs cooked the macaroni until soft, then probably coated it with butter and added cheese. The mixture was then possibly dotted with more butter and cheese and baked until it was golden brown with some crustiness on top.

Machiavelli Macaroni and Cheese

Ingredients:

16 ounces large elbow macaroni
3 cups milk
2 teaspoons all-purpose flour
½ teaspoon salt
2 cups freshly shredded Parmesan (packed)
2 cups grated mozzarella (packed)
2 cups grated Romano or Gruyère cheese (packed)
2 tablespoons butter
Salt and pepper to taste

Yield: Serves 6 to 8

Directions:

Preheat the oven to 425°F. Butter a 13 x 9-inch glass baking dish and set aside. In a large pot of boiling water, cook the noodles until soft, 6 to 8 minutes. Drain but don't rinse.

In a large bowl, whisk the milk, flour, and salt until

blended. Stir in 1½ cups Parmesan, 1½ cups mozzarella, and 1½ cups Romano (or Gruyère) cheese. Add the noodles and butter. Toss to coat. Transfer the noodle mixture to the prepared baking dish. Sprinkle the remaining Parmesan, mozzarella, and Romano (or Gruyère) cheese over the noodle mixture. Bake until the cheese begins to lightly brown on top, 12 to 14 minutes. Let stand for 5 to 10 minutes before serving. Season with salt and pepper to taste and enjoy!

SELECT BIBLIOGRAPHY

Several excellent biographies of Machiavelli have appeared in recent years, among the best of these being Miles J. Unger's engaging and accessible *Machiavelli: A Biography* (New York: Simon & Schuster, 2011); Maurizio Viroli's *Niccolò's Smile: A Biography of Machiavelli* (New York: Farrar, Straus and Giroux, 2000); Quentin Skinner's *Machiavelli: A Very Short Introduction* (Oxford, UK: Oxford University Press, 2000); Ross King's *Machiavelli: Philosopher of Power* (New York: Atlas Books/HarperCollins, 2007); and Sebastian De Grazia's Pulitzer Prize–winning *Machiavelli in Hell* (Princeton, NJ: Princeton University Press, 1989).

A vast and ever-growing literature exists on Machiavelli's political thought, with the most influential work being

J. G. A. Pocock's classic *The Machiavellian Moment: Florentine Political Thought and the Atlantic Republican Tradition* (Princeton, NJ: Princeton University Press, 1975); J. G. A. Pocock, *"The Machiavellian Moment* Revisited: A Study in History and Ideology," *Journal of Modern History* 53, no. 1 (March 1981): 49–72; John M. Najemy, ed., *The Cambridge Companion to Machiavelli* (Cambridge: Cambridge University Press, 2010); Gisela Bock, Quentin Skinner, and Maurizio Viroli, eds., *Machiavelli and Republicanism* (Cambridge: Cambridge University Press, 1990); and Paul A. Rahe, ed., *Machiavelli's Liberal Republican Legacy* (Cambridge: Cambridge University Press, 2006); and Peter Bondanella, Mark Musa, eds., *The Portable Machiavelli* (New York: Penguin Books, 1979).

For more lighthearted takes on how Machiavelli's advice can be applied to modern-day life, see Stanley Bing's rollicking *What Would Machiavelli Do? The Ends Justify the Meanness* (New York: HarperBusiness, 2000), and *Strategy Power Plays: Winning Business Ideas from the World's Greatest Strategic Minds* (Oxford: Infinite Ideas, 2009) by Karen McCreadie, Tim Phillips, and Steve Shipside. Other useful sources include:

Atkinson, James B. "Niccoló Machiavelli: A Portrait." In *The Cambridge Companion to Machiavelli*, ed. John M. Najemy. Cambridge: Cambridge University Press, 2010.

Barthas, Jérémie. "Machiavelli in Political Thought from the Age of Revolutions to the Present." In *The Cambridge Companion to Machiavelli*, ed. John M. Najemy. Cambridge: Cambridge University Press, 2010.

Berlin, Isaiah. "The Question of Machiavelli." *New York Review of Books*, November 4, 1971.

Black, Robert. "Machiavelli, Servant of the Florentine Republic." In *Machiavelli and Republicanism*, ed. Gisela Bock, Quentin Skinner, and Maurizio Viroli. Cambridge: Cambridge University Press, 1990.

The Comedy and Tragedy of Machiavelli: Essays on the Literary Works. Edited by Vickie B. Sullivan. New Haven, CT: Yale University Press, 2000.

Deitz, Mary. "Trapping the Prince: Machiavelli and the Politics of Deception." *American Political Science Review* 80, no. 3 (September 1986): 777–91.

Donskis, Leonidas, ed., *Niccolò Machiavelli: History, Power, and Virtue*, Amsterdam: Rodopi, 2011.

Fischer, Markus. "Machiavelli's Political Psychology." *Review of Politics* 59, no. 4 (Autumn 1997): 789–829.

Gilbert, Felix. "Machiavelli: The Renaissance of the Art of War." In Edward Mead Earle, ed., *Makers of Modern Strategy*. Princeton, NJ: Princeton University Press, 1944.

Guarini, Elena. "Machiavelli and the Crisis of the Italian Republics." In *Machiavelli and Republicanism*, ed. Gisela Bock, Quentin Skinner, and Maurizio Viroli. Cambridge: Cambridge University Press, 1990.

Macaulay, Thomas. "Machiavelli." In *English Essays: Sidney to Macaulay*. Vol. 27 of *The Harvard Classics*. New York: Collier, 1910.

Machiavelli Niccolò. *Machiavelli and His Friends: Their Personal Correspondence*. Edited by James B. Atkinson and David Sices. DeKalb: Northern Illinois University Press, 1996.

Mansfield, Harvey. "Machiavelli and the Idea of Progress." In *History and the Idea of Progress*, ed. Arthur M. Melzer, Jerry

Weinberger, and M. Richard Zinman. Ithaca, NY: Cornell University Press, 1995.

———. "Machiavelli's Political Science." *American Political Science Review* 75, no. 2 (June 1981): 293–305.

———. *Machiavelli's Virtue.* Chicago: University of Chicago Press, 1996.

———. *Taming the Prince.* Baltimore: Johns Hopkins University Press, 1993.

Masters, Roger D. *Fortune Is a River: Leonardo Da Vinci and Niccolò Machiavelli's Magnificent Dream to Change the Course of Florentine History.* New York: Free Press, 1998.

———. *Machiavelli, Leonardo and the Science of Power.* Notre Dame, IN: University of Notre Dame Press, 1996.

Mattingly, Garrett. "Machiavelli's *Prince*: Political Science or Political Satire?" *American Scholar* 27, no. 4 (Autumn 1958): 482–91.

Najemy, John M. "Baron's Machiavelli and Renaissance Republicanism." *American Historical Review* 101, no. 1 (February 1996): 119–29.

———. *Between Friends: Discourses of Power and Desire in the Machiavelli-Vettori Letters of 1513–1515.* Princeton, NJ: Princeton University Press, 1993.

Nederman, Cary. "Niccolò Machiavelli." In *Stanford Encyclopedia of Philosophy* (Fall 2009), ed. Edward N. Zalta, http:plato.stanford .edu/archives/fall2009/entries/machiavelli.

Parel, A. J. "The Question of Machiavelli's Modernity." *Review of Politics* 53, no. 2 (Spring 1991): 320–39.

Pierpont, Claudia Roth. "The Man Who Taught Rulers How to Rule." *New Yorker*, September 15, 2008.

Pitkin, Hanna. *Fortune Is a Woman.* Berkeley: University of California Press, 1984.

Ridolfi, Roberto. *The Life of Niccolò Machiavelli.* Trans. Cecil Grayson. Chicago: University of Chicago Press, 1963.

Skinner, Quentin. *The Foundations of Modern Political Thought.* Volume 1, *The Renaissance.* Cambridge: Cambridge University Press, 1978.

———. *Machiavelli: A Very Short Introduction.* Oxford, UK: Oxford University Press, 2006.

Soll, Jacob. *Publishing* The Prince*: History, Reading, and the Birth of Political Criticism.* Ann Arbor: University of Michigan Press, 2005.

Strauss, Leo. "Niccolò Machiavelli." In *History of Political Philosophy,* 3rd ed., edited by Leo Strauss and Joseph Cropsey. Chicago: University of Chicago Press, 1987.

———. *Thoughts on Machiavelli.* Glencoe, IL: Free Press, 1958.

Wood, Neal. "Introduction." In Niccolò Machiavelli, *The Art of War,* a revised edition of the Ellis Farneworthe translation. New York: Da Capo Press, 2001.

ACKNOWLEDGMENTS

The wheel of fortune turned decisively my way when I crossed paths with Joy Tutela of the David Black Literary Agency. Since then, she has been an enthusiastic advocate for this book and has made each stage of its creation enjoyable, rewarding, and fun. So "*grazie!*" my friend. It has been and is a pleasure working with you.

Many thanks also to my unbelievably talented and tireless editor at Simon & Schuster/Touchstone, Michelle Howry, whose vision for this book shaped it from its inception and whose contributions helped turn it into what it is, and to the rest of the Touchstone team: Stacy Creamer, David Falk, Marcia Burch, Jessica Roth, Sally Kim, Lisa Healy, and Kiele Raymond. Special thanks, too, to Cherlynne Li for the fun cover. Love the boots!

At UC Berkeley: thanks to David Hollinger and Margaret Lavinia Anderson for your patience and support at a time when I needed it the most.

Closer to home: deep thanks to my parents for putting up with my childhood shenanigans and for teaching me by example that strict but fair discipline always inures to the benefit of a child, even though I might not have agreed at the time. Many thanks also to my husband, Eric Woods, for always making me laugh and holding my hand on our journey together through parenthood. Of course, my deepest and most heartfelt thanks go to my sweet, beautiful, funny, loving, kind, and (mostly) well-behaved kids. You guys might drive me crazy sometimes but *nothing* makes me happier or prouder than being your mom!

Finally: a grateful smile and nod of acknowledgment to Machiavelli for helping me reclaim my kingdom and without whom this book literally would not have been possible.

Un sentito ringraziamento a tutti!

ABOUT THE AUTHOR

Suzanne Evans is a former divorce lawyer and business reporter who holds a PhD in history from UC Berkeley. Her first nonfiction book is *Forgotten Crimes: The Holocaust and People with Disabilities.* Her work has also appeared in the *New York Times,* the *Los Angeles Times,* the *Los Angeles Business Journal* (where she was a staff reporter), and other national publications. A former freelance writer for the History Channel Web site, she is also the creator of *The History Chef,* a popular food history blog for parents and kids.